ESCAPING
THE BLITZ

Best wishes,

Penny Legg

ESCAPING THE BLITZ

THE MYTHS & MAYHEM OF EVACUATION IN THE SECOND WORLD WAR

Penny Starns & Penny Legg

SABRESTORM

In memory of Peter Legg
(1932 – 1987)
WW2 Evacuee

Designed and typeset by Philip Clucas MSIAD

British Library Cataloguing in Publication Data

A catalogue record for this book is available
from the British Library

Published by Sabrestorm Publishing,
The Olive Branch, Caen Hill, Devizes,
Wiltshire SN10 1RB

Website: *www.sabrestorm.com*

Email: *books@sabrestorm.com*

ISBN 9781781220177

Contents

Acknowledgements

There are always many people to thank when writing a book. We hope that we have remembered everyone. If not, we apologise and thank you now.

This book would not have come to be if it were not for Dianne Partridge, who organises an annual reunion for wartime evacuees, held in Southampton. She listened to the stories these now elderly ladies and gentlemen told, and felt that their experiences should not be forgotten. Some of these have been combined with background information on the story of the WW2 evacuations to make this book. Thank you, Dianne.

Ian Bayley of Sabrestorm Publishing, who loved the idea of a new book on evacuees, this time with associated video to bring the printed words alive. Thank you, Ian.

The staff and members of The British Evacuees Association.

Members of the Birmingham Evacuee Association.

Archivists across the country have assisted our research efforts and we would like to express our gratitude to the archivists based at the Imperial War Museum and those working in local record offices across the UK.

Liz Bosanko, who interviewed the late Ted Stubbington just before his death to ensure that his memories were recorded for posterity. Thank you, Liz.

Thank you to the evacuees who shared their experiences over welcome cups of tea, or who sent the authors their stories:

Kathy Avagah	Doris Nicholson (née Cook)
Jean and Raymond Banks	Peter Nobes
Mary-Rose Benton	Ken Oakley
John Bowen	Enid Philpott
George Burt	'Pat'
Dennis Edward Carrett	Terence Randall
Patricia Carrett	The late Jill Simmonds (née Eliott)
Alan Corbishley	The late Ted Stubbington
Tony Edwards	May Toone
John Henry Grant Evans	John Virgo
Jack Flanagan	Roy Webb
Janet and John Hammond	Dee Williams
Peter Mooney	

Special thanks to the hundreds of evacuees and their teachers for contributing to the University of Cambridge History of Evacuation Project, and the ESRC for funding this research.

Thanks, too, to Christine Donovan and Patricia Soares for all their support and to Thomas Legg, who filmed some of the interviews so that they were kept for posterity.

Last, but definitely not least, thanks to Joe Legg, whose late father Peter this book is dedicated to.

A note from Penny Legg

It was a pleasure to interview and film many evacuees and I am so grateful for their permissions to include the content in this book. I apologise if not all the interviews made it into the final version, but I had so many wonderful stories to include I had to leave some bits out. Time dims even the sharpest mind, so please bear with the story teller if their version of events does not quite fit with the view given in the history books.

QR Codes and online content

Throughout this book we have incorporated QR codes like the one here, that link to short video clips of some of those evacuees interviewed. The QR code is a type of barcode that can be scanned by a smartphone and links to the specific video. You will need the appropriate technology and web access to view these clips and whilst these videos are not essential to the enjoyment of the book we hope they will enhance your satisfaction.

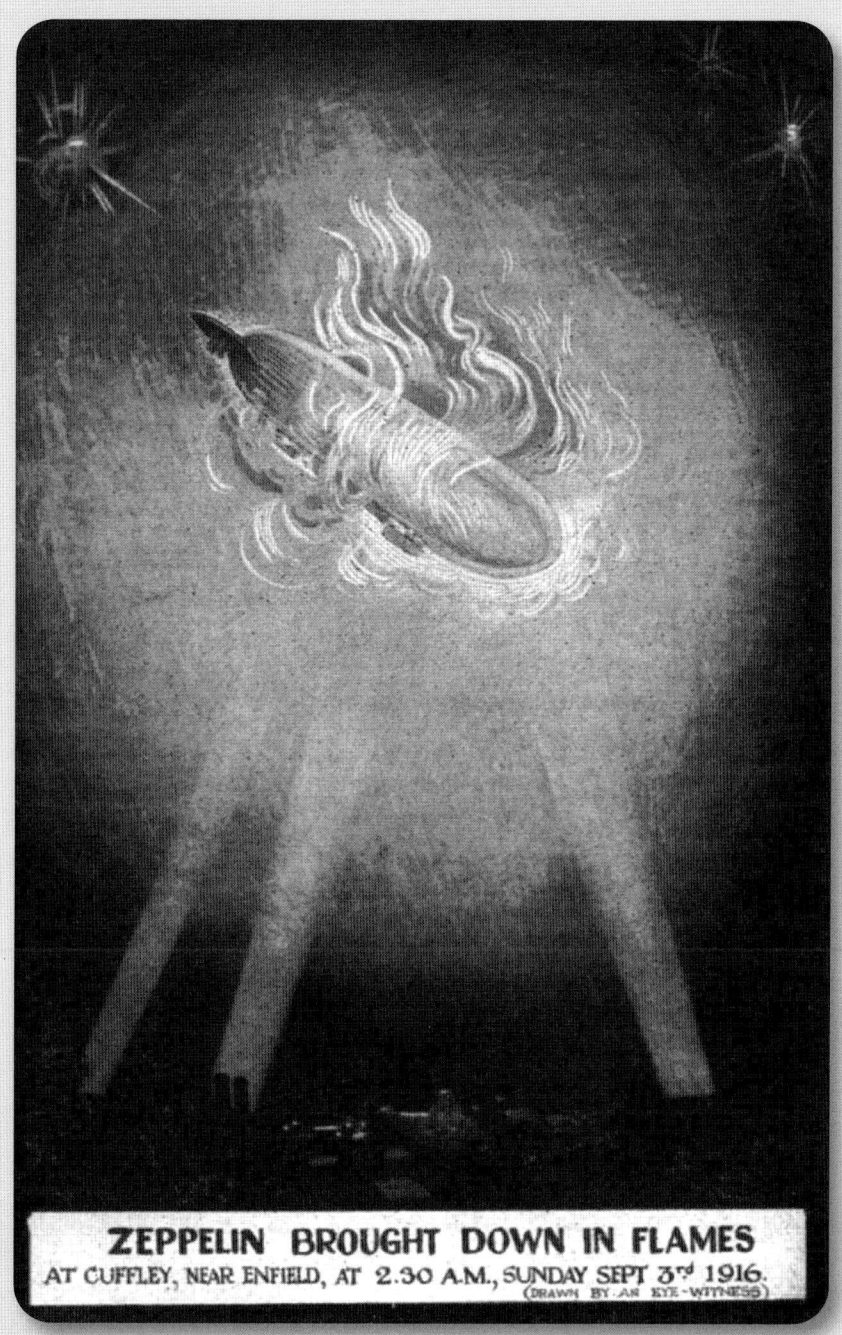

Above: This WW1 postcard illustrates the new wartime
danger of Zeppelin raids on the civilian population.

Introduction

Why were children sent into exile during World War Two?

In the first three days of the aptly-named Operation Pied Piper over one and a half million children were evacuated from towns, cities and seaports deemed by the government to be most at risk of enemy bombardment: Edinburgh, Glasgow, Newcastle, Leeds, Liverpool, Manchester, Birmingham, Portsmouth and London. From London alone, 240,000 children were evacuated (Simon Smith). Children were uprooted from their homes and taken to places of near-safety, most notably to rural communities, to live with complete strangers. Over 100,000 teachers were sent with them as 'handlers' (*Daily Mail*). Mothers and expectant women were also evacuated, as were some 23,000 civil servants, who found themselves working in spa towns or along the coast, away from the danger of an expected blitz. This massive undertaking, in three waves in 1939, 1940 and 1944, the biggest migration the country has ever known, was a planned event, but what led to the government taking such a step?

Technical advances had been making giant strides since the rickety days of the first fatal Zeppelin raid during World War One, when two people were killed and three injured in East Anglia on 19 January 1915. By 1916, when aeroplanes had the ability to shoot down the Zeppelin, there were 556 dead and 1300 injured, many from London but also from other strategically important towns across the country. Aeroplanes in groups began to bombard Britain and, by 1918, 1413 civilians had been killed, almost half of them from London. Plans for the evacuation of civilians from towns were drawn up but the war was over before they could be refined and implemented. Planning continued sluggishly during the 1920s and 30s. It was the widespread aerial bombardment of Barcelona during the 1936 Spanish Civil War that highlighted the need for effective civil defence measures. By the outbreak of the Second World War, plans for the evacuation of children and vulnerable adults were in place.

Escaping the Blitz is the story of the biggest social upheaval in British history. Portrayed by the government as a positive by-product of the Second World War, civilian evacuation formed an essential part of Britain's civil defence strategy. In a single stroke, children were uprooted from their close-knit family communities and replanted in unfamiliar and sometimes hostile surroundings. This totally haphazard mingling of social classes had profound and long-lasting effects on British society. Education, health, welfare, religion and social policy were all re-evaluated in the light of evacuation. From a government standpoint, evacuation was an exercise in military logistics. For those who took part however, it was a life changing experience. Furthermore, there was no typical evacuee experience, only a shared sense of alienation in the face of adversity. Some evacuees were lucky enough to have positive and uplifting encounters, while others less fortunate suffered physical, emotional and sexual abuse.

Apart from the myth that all evacuees spent the war years having a wonderful time in the country, there were other tales of evacuation that were told with a certain amount of relish throughout the post-war decades. According to these tales, evacuees did not know how to use a knife and fork, were unable to go to the toilet in the appropriate place, could not read or write, nor wash or clean their teeth. These stories were grossly exaggerated to highlight the problems of some host families, yet they serve to form a stereotypical picture of the evacuee that is perpetuated in literature, the media and even the national school curriculum.

Stereotypes of evacuee behaviour in history are only surpassed by stereotypes of the British people in wartime. The notion, for instance, that everyone pulled together as a whole in the face of a common enemy was sustained in the popular press despite considerable evidence to the contrary. Black market racketeering, bribery and corruption were all prominent features of wartime Britain, contributing to an overall rise in the home-front crime rate of fifty-seven per cent.

Evacuees were not just sent to British safe-spots. They found themselves on ships bound for Canada, New Zealand, South Africa, Australia and the United States of America before the sinking of the SS City of Benares in 1940, and the loss of seventy-seven of the ninety children on board, forced such overseas evacuations to stop. Children who were sent abroad were used by central government for propaganda purposes. They were groomed to act as ambassadors for Britain, and government policy in this respect was largely dictated by the international situation. Overseas evacuation was, amongst other things, an attempt to elicit international financial support for the war effort and persuade America to join the war on the side of the allies.

Apart from their role as ambassadors, British children carried a further responsibility. They were essential for the survival of the British race, and overseas evacuation policy reflected this concern.

Above: This image graphically illustrates the fear in every parent's mind.
This fear was a prime motivation for many parents to evacuate their children.

Life as an evacuee came in all manner of shapes and sizes, from those sent to live in local manor houses, to those finding themselves in cottages or on farms. For city kids, life on a farm came as a surprise, open fields and large animals being unknowns in their lives to that point. Older boys found themselves the favourites of farmers, who chose to billet them because they would be able to work in the fields. Public perceptions of children however, shifted throughout the war. In 1939, children were either viewed as innocents in need of protection, or as useless mouths who were draining the nation of vital food supplies. Yet, by 1941, they had become active participants in the war effort, and children as young as five could be found working on the land. By 1943, the Ministry of Agriculture and Fisheries considered children to be a vital component of Britain's food production industry. This remained so, long after the war ended.

Those taking in evacuees received 10 shillings and six pence per week for the first and eight shillings and six pence for each subsequent child. Some took in children because they wished to help but others had less pure intentions and many stories surfaced of neglect and abuse by those whose only interest was the additional income for taking evacuees in. Allocation was often by the simple means of lining up the children to be looked over. Their prospective guardians viewed those on offer and made their choice saying, "I'll take that one."

Evacuation policy violated the child's right to be with family and community, and from that basic violation all other rights were denied. In some cases, evacuation even violated the right to life, since there were children who died as a direct result of evacuation. Some of those who were evacuated to Bath, for instance, died as a result of bombing. Others died as a result of neglect, ill-treatment or a lack of supervision in the reception areas. Two children evacuated from Glasgow died on the Solway Shore, for example, during the first two weeks of evacuation. (Hansard House of Commons Debates 5th Series 14 September 1939, col 878). For all its obvious violations of children's rights, evacuation policy has never been seriously questioned. Traditional histories of the Second World War have portrayed evacuation as both desirable and necessary when in fact it was neither. It was merely the cheapest option. Evacuation occurred because the British government did not invest in adequate civil defence measures, and because labour and military concerns took precedence over those of child safety.

This book looks at the waves of internal evacuation and at the experiences of those 'sea-vacs' who were sent abroad. Using previously unpublished reminiscences from those who were evacuated, the authors seek to shed new light on the government's policy of dispersal and to show what life was like for the evacuees when they returned home.

Penny Starns and Penny Legg

Right: The government could not stop the consequences of a blitz but could take steps to send the vulnerable to relative safety.

Escaping the Blitz
Prologue

'No one told you much.'

John Bowen, evacuated from Southampton, aged six

Anyone who has ever read Robert Browning's *Pied Piper of Hamelin* will remember that most of the children in the fairy tale disappeared inside a mountain as a result of following the Pied Piper. Nevertheless, this gruesome tale did not deter the British Government from choosing 'Operation Pied Piper' as the official code name for its civilian evacuation scheme of 1939. Plans for a civilian evacuation in the event of a future war were discussed as early as 1922 and the issue was resurrected again in 1932, but nothing concrete was set in motion until 1938. In this year, a Sub-Committee of the Imperial Defence Committee was established under the chairmanship of Sir John Anderson to examine the logistics of civilian evacuation in more detail.

From the First World War and through the experiences of the aerial bombing of Barcelona during the Spanish Civil War, British politicians were aware that any future war would be fought in the air, and consequently the risks to civilians would come in the form of aerial attacks. Thus, the original remit of the Anderson Committee suggested that members should merely look at the ways in which people who were considered to be at risk of sustained aerial attacks could be transported to less vulnerable areas. From the outset, committee members acknowledged that in a country the size of Britain it was impossible to guarantee total safety to any member of the population. Therefore, government evacuation policy concentrated on the 'dispersal' of the population, a term which could by no means be equated with 'safety'. The dispersal policy simply meant that less people were likely to be bombed in any one city or county because the population was dispersed over a wider geographical area. Government ministers referred to evacuation in terms of relative safety but never of total safety.

The Spanish Civil War had highlighted the problems associated with large scale civilian evacuations, and demonstrated the enormous value of deep shelters, which allowed families to stay together. Lieutenant-Colonel Sir Mervyn Manningham-Buller suggested that building costs could be reduced by utilising such shelters in Britain as car parks.[1]

However, Britain's ministers chose to send the Under-Secretary of State to Berlin in order to ascertain the proposed German plans for civil defence. This action was highly criticised in the House of Commons. Mr Lansbury MP asked with some indignation:

In view of the Alice in Wonderland sort of arrangement come to between the Under-Secretary of State and the authorities in Berlin for him to go there and – I understand that he has been there - does the Right Hon. Gentleman think that the public will have any confidence in this business in view of the fact that the Under-Secretary was sent to Berlin to find out how the German government will protect their people against our bombing – and that he was sent there to enquire from them how we should protect ourselves against the possibility of their bombing us? If that is not the height and depth of tomfoolery, I do not know what is.[2]

Yet, despite substantial evidence from Spain and the persuasive arguments put forward by some ministers in the House of Commons in favour of building deep shelters as an alternative to evacuation, the idea failed to gain support. Some MPs believed that civilians would take to living underground on a permanent basis, while others argued that such large shelters would become the subject of gas attacks. But the overriding objection to the plan was financial. Government ministers were simply not prepared to invest in the building of such shelters when dispersal was a far cheaper option.

Civil defence plans were also dictated by practical considerations. Government officials were all too aware that, when it came to maintaining essential war industries an 'all hands on deck' approach was needed. Naturally, a full-scale evacuation of children liberated more women for war work by relieving them of their maternal duties.

Military morale was another high priority. Commanding officers argued that members of the armed forces would not fight effectively unless they knew that their children had been evacuated. Furthermore, some military advisers maintained that major cities were likely to become actual fields of combat and children were bound to obstruct the fighting. Worse still, they could be taken hostage by the enemy in an attempt to force a British surrender.

As planning progressed, a public information leaflet issued by the Lord Privy Seal's office in July 1939 expressed the government view succinctly:

The purpose of evacuation is to remove from the crowded and vulnerable centres, if an emergency should arise, those, more particularly children, whose presence cannot be of any assistance.[3]

Along with children, pregnant women, cripples, blind, deaf and the sick were also viewed as useless and were included in the proposed evacuation scheme.

The Anderson Committee on Evacuation, headed by the workaholic Sir John Anderson, chiefly remembered for the Anderson Shelter, the make-shift bomb shelter at the bottom of many gardens, worked hard to construct an evacuation scheme that would work like clockwork. Committee members drew up distinct lines across the British landscape, dividing Britain into evacuation, reception and neutral areas.

Video 1 Janet Hammond: *Life in an air raid shelter*

Military advice, although sought, was often not heeded. On 28 June 1938, for example, the Anderson Committee sought the advice of Wing Commander R V Goddard of the Air Staff. The prospect of air attacks and the importance of strategic evacuation areas were discussed at length. Goddard advised the committee members to evacuate civilians to counties west of London rather than to the east, since bombers were more likely to attack the east coast of Britain. When Operation Pied Piper was implemented, however, the Anderson Committee chose to ignore Goddard's view and evacuate children to the east regardless of the potential danger. Consequently, some children in the early stages of the war experienced more bombing after their evacuation than they would have done if they had remained in London. It was a policy that also led to more upheaval for those who had to be evacuated again when the war came to the east coast.

Video 2 George Burt: *The practice evacuation*

Practice evacuation sessions were set up at some schools before war was declared. George Burt, aged seven when he was evacuated from Calvert Road School, Greenwich, first to Hastings and then to Whitland in West Wales, remembers: *'We practiced a week before the declaration of war because they realised possibly the Germans would not go along with what Neville Chamberlain was going to say. I was only seven years, four months then but I can remember us having to go in crocodiles of children. We had a gas mask and a little case or bag, and we had a label round our neck with our name and address on.'[4]*

For most of the country's evacuees, a plan was devised which utilised a combination of underground and above-ground trains and buses. In London, the underground system was used to take children to main railway termini where they either caught buses or other trains. In other parts of the country, children were transported from suburban railway lines to the main termini.

One hundred and sixty-four Great Western trains were allotted the task of ferrying evacuees from the designated stations of Paddington, Ealing and Acton and sixty-four were assigned to remove children from Birmingham. Great Western and other railway companies also ferried children from other towns and cities.[5]

In their early deliberations, members of the Anderson Committee had decided that children should be evacuated with their school teachers and billeted in private homes in the countryside. Although thirty-one purpose-built camp schools were later constructed, in terms of housing large numbers of evacuee school children, private billeting was by far the cheapest option for the government. Teachers also endorsed this system of private billeting because they did not particularly want to assume total responsibility for their pupils.

In order to establish the number of rooms which could be made available to evacuees, volunteer visitors were appointed in all the proposed reception areas. In January 1939, these visitors scoured the countryside, visiting five million homes, noting the types of accommodation available and the willingness of potential host families to open their doors to evacuees. They were also required to note the distance of accommodation from schools and villages. This survey revealed that 18 percent of the available billeting had already been earmarked by private evacuees seven months before the outbreak of war.[6] At no point in this survey did anyone ask questions of the potential hosts as to their suitability to care for children. Indeed, throughout the war, no character checks were ever made on the receiving hosts, nor did the government

Video 3 Janet Hammond: *Private evacuation*

establish a monitoring system to ensure the physical and emotional safety of evacuees. This fundamental oversight caused immense suffering to many children.

This was in direct contrast to the 'Movement for the Care of Children from Germany', for example, which had laid down specific guidelines for the placement of refugee children who had arrived in Britain to escape Nazi persecution. Potential hosts were screened by their religion, social position, marital status, financial status, educational views, religious options for the child, views on training and general views on the upbringing of children. Further, interviewers entered the homes of potential hosts and ascertained the proposed sleeping arrangements for the child and warned them that a member of the organisation's committee would visit the home unexpectedly from time to time to ensure the well-being of the child in their care.[7]

The government chose to make billeting compulsory. Certain categories of potential hosts, such as those who were disabled or chronically sick, were initially exempt, but eventually the pressure to find billets was too great and nobody could escape the prospect of looking after lively children, regardless of their age or disability. However, although billeting was made compulsory, evacuation was not, and no reception area had any idea of the numbers of evacuees they were likely to receive. There was also some confusion over which organisations were responsible not only for the evacuation process but also for the safety of the children once they were evacuated.

Initially, the Home Office had assumed responsibility for the whole evacuation scheme. There were genuine concerns within government circles that civilians would leave cities in a blind panic once war broke out, or in the case of London, it was assumed they would take to the underground and live a subterranean existence for the duration of the war. Therefore, the Home Office was given the responsibility of ensuring an orderly evacuation of civilians. In a political move designed to appeal to parents, the responsibility for evacuation was shifted to the Ministry of Health on 14 November 1938. It was felt that parents would be more likely to send their children into the reception areas if the scheme was run by health ministers rather than those associated with the Home Office. Nevertheless, some confusion remained. In the end, it was the people employed by the Board of Education who were destined to be the lynchpin of the whole scheme.

Teachers had experience of child crowd control and, Anderson reasoned, children were most likely to follow the instructions of their teachers in the event of an emergency. Following discussions between the Anderson Committee and teacher representatives, the National Union of Teachers voluntarily resolved to co-operate with government plans for an evacuation, although teachers did voice concerns about whether or not evacuation should be made compulsory.

Following much deliberation and heated debate, the Anderson Committee rejected the idea of compulsory evacuation. Neither Anderson nor any other committee member wanted to be accused of adopting the measures of their fascist enemy and believed that, with some gentle persuasion, parents would eventually support the scheme. However, government ministers were not particularly good at the art of persuasion, gentle or otherwise, and most lacked any degree of emotional empathy with the parents of prospective evacuees. This lack of empathy can be attributed to some extent to the gender gap, or perhaps to the fact that some politicians were not parents. However, some ministers failed to empathise with the average working-class housewife, primarily because of class difference. They themselves had been brought up in upper-class households where it was perfectly acceptable for children to be packed off to boarding school at an early age and, quite honestly, they could not see what the fuss was about. Dr Edith Summerskill summed up the case to the Minister of Health in the House of Commons:

> *'I feel that the government have not realised the fundamental psychological problem which confronts them. Let me remind the Minister of the life of a working-class housewife. Her life has been one of drudgery from the time she got married, and when she thinks upon her life, her only compensation, the only thing that makes her say, 'well it has been worthwhile,' is for her to look at her children. She has created them; she has fed them. In all those homes, her life revolves around her children. Surely, then, the Minister should ask himself what is the best way to reach a mother.'*[8]

Summerskill's pleas for a compassionate approach to mothers fell on deaf ears. More emphasis on the emotional problems most mothers faced when confronting the prospect of parting from their children might have resulted in a greater turn out for the actual event. The government was asking parents to send their children quite literally into the unknown. It was not unreasonable, therefore, for parents to demand some reassurance.

Not surprisingly, government disregard for parental concern was reflected in the parental response to evacuation. As Operation Pied Piper swung into action, the numbers of evacuees fell dramatically short of government expectations. Even though 1,500,000 children were moved from their city homes to rural areas over a period of three days, this number amounted to only 47 percent of English school children and 38 percent of Scottish school children.

Each wave of evacuation was accompanied by persistent problems in the reception areas and a lack of parental faith in government assurances. The decision to opt for voluntary rather than compulsory evacuation was also a recipe for disaster, since reception areas were never entirely sure of how many children to expect. Officials in Whitehall systematically failed to equip the rural areas adequately for the arrival of vast numbers of children and at no time during the war did any government minister visit any of the reception areas. Operation Pied Piper ran like clockwork if viewed in terms of offloading the responsibility of evacuees from central government onto local authorities. Once the evacuees had reached their destination, however, an unprecedented and agonisingly prolonged chaos descended upon both rural and urban reception areas.

Endnotes

1 Hansard House of Commons Debates 5th Series 3 March 1938, col 1264
2 Hansard House of Commons Debates 5th Series 3 February 1938, col 362
3 *Evacuation Why and How* - Public Information Leaflet no3, issued by the Lod Privy Seal's Office, July 1939
4 Interview with George Burt, 2017
5 Bryan, T., *Great Western Railway at War* (1995) pp. 10-16
6 Parsons, M., *I'll Take That One* (Peterborough, 1998) p.56
7 *Instructions for the Guidance of Regional and Local Committees – The Executive Committee of the Movement for the Care of Children from Germany,* May 1940 p.11 Herefordshire County Record Office J65/1406
8 Hansard Debates, *House of Commons*, 5th series, June 15, 1940, col 411-454

Chapter 1
Evacuation 1939

*"You're not suggesting that I take these children
into my house?"*

Eglantine Price, *Bedknobs and Broomsticks* (Played by Angela Lansbury, Disney, 1971)

On 31 August 1939, the British government ended months of suspense and practice runs by issuing the order to 'evacuate forthwith'. Parents, teachers, helpers, transport officials and voluntary services leapt into action to implement an exodus of biblical proportions. In England, official figures record that 673,000 unaccompanied school children, 406,000 mothers and young children and 3,000 expectant mothers were moved during the course of three days. In Scotland, the figure was estimated at 175,000 persons, of which 50,000 were unaccompanied children.[1]

Video 4 George Bert: *Bewilderment*

For most of the evacuees it was a time of bewilderment. Some had been told that they were going on a long holiday, others an adventure. Few were told the real reason for their departure. Children were allowed to take very little with them when they left. The list was austere due to a lack of space on the trains carrying them, many of which were without seating or toilets:

Gas mask; a change of underclothing; night clothes; spare shoes or plimsolls; spare stockings or socks; a toothbrush and comb; knife, fork and spoon; mug and plate; towel and handkerchief; a warm coat or mackintosh; a day's food.

The list was not always attainable by some poorer families, for whom, for example, the delights of a warm coat or a waterproof mackintosh were an out-of-reach luxury.

Video 5 Janet Hammond: *Gas masks*

School children congregated at their respective schools early in the morning with their meagre belongings, before commencing their long haul to the reception areas. Trains began to depart from 8.30 am onwards. Jean Banks was almost twelve when she and her two sisters were evacuated from the Swaythling area of Southampton, via Southampton Central railway station, to Dorchester. She remembers the train that carried them to Poole Parkway, where buses were waiting to take them on the next leg of their journey. She says, 'The train was full of London evacuees, half of them crying. Every carriage was packed with children.' Jean's mother had put her clothes and those of her seven-year-old sister Doreen into carrier bags, which caused problems almost immediately.

Video 6 Jean Banks: *No toys*

Video 7 Jean Banks: *Going on the train*

'It was a very wet day, pouring with rain. We only had carrier bags. They were paper. They got wetter and wetter and wetter. They had our change of clothes in there; that's all we could take. They were disintegrating. So, I said to my sister, Doreen,

Video 8 Jean Banks: *Paper carrier bag*

Video 9 Ray Banks: *Evacuation journey*

"Well, what we had better do...I'll take my coat off and lay it on the ground. You put your underwear and change of clothes on top of mine in the coat." I then tied the arms together to make a bag of it. I discarded the carrier bags, they had fallen apart.'[2]

The Avagah family were typical of those evacuated to the east coast. They were moved from Dagenham, which was not originally designated as an evacuation area. It was later added after lobbying by Dagenham Borough Council, the Press and local people. Consequently, arrangements for the onward dispersal of evacuees from the area did not begin until June 1939, by which time most of the available transport had already been booked.

Kathy Avagah notes how she and her family were evacuated.

'Over two days, starting before dawn broke on Friday 1 September 1939, the evacuees assembled in various schools in Dagenham. Whilst it was still dark they started to be ferried, or if they were unlucky, marched, to the gates of the Ford Motor Company's works. Waiting at the Ford jetties,

which jut out into the River Thames, were paddle-steamers belonging to the General Steam Navigation Company, which were usually used for cross-channel work.

'With the help of the Ford workers, who carried the smaller children the long distance from the gates to the jetty, the embarkation began. When each boat was full it edged out into the river to make its way down-stream, past Tilbury, Gravesend and Southend and then out to sea. My father had volunteered for the Army, leaving Mum in Dagenham with seven children aged from 14 months to 13-years-old. With two children under five my mother was evacuated with us.'³

A teacher from Dagenham also recalled the exodus:

'The school was still being lit by gas and that holiday they had been ripping out all the gas fittings and they hadn't got round to fitting up the electricity because obviously, it was still summer and we wouldn't need any lighting for a couple of months. So, the morning that we all assembled it was absolutely dark. I had two candles on my desk to mark off the register of the people who said they were going. The children were at the desks with their bags and you couldn't really distinguish who was just saying goodbye to their loved ones and who were coming with us. I can remember so vividly the darkness outside and all the faces peering in of poor souls who had had to make this decision to send their children.

'… a lot of them hadn't got toothbrushes or facecloths or towels or anything, because they were family things and they were finding great problems in getting their clothes together. When they arrived on the Friday, they got all sorts of bags and cases and anything they could get hold of to put their stuff in. When we finally set off from school it was moonlight and we walked through the streets of Dagenham down to the docks. It was all very calm. It was a great adventure you see. We didn't know where we were going and it was exciting because a lot of these children could never have had a holiday.'⁴

Ken Oakley echoes this excitement. His first memory of the morning he was evacuated from Southampton to Bournemouth as a seven-year-old was how he was going to get there:

'I remember walking towards the train – Cor, going on a train ride! All I remember was that we were going away and that was exciting.'⁵

For John Bowen, evacuated from Southampton to Bournemouth, things were slightly different:

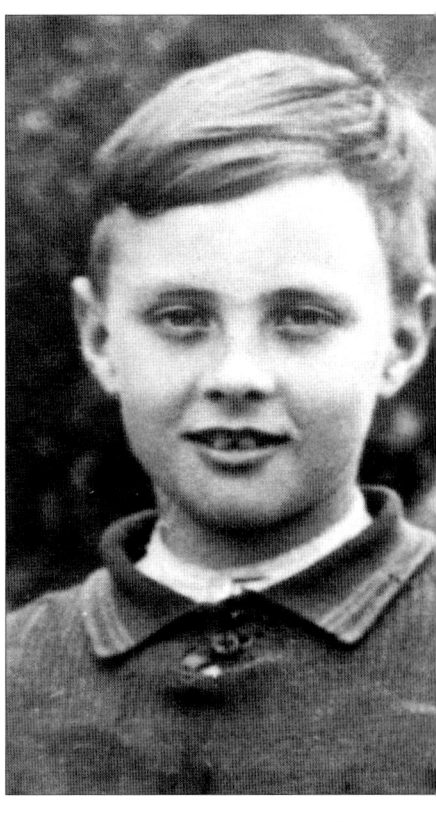

Right: John Bowen, aged 9, evacuated to Somerset. This photograph was taken in 1941. On the reverse he has written: For five years never saw my family until I came back. I was evacuated to Charlton Musgrove in Somerset.

'I was six coming up to 7. We thought we were just going for a few days. No one told you much, you know. We thought it won't be long.

'I remember getting up one morning early and my sister getting me ready. It was pitch black. We walked up to Springhill School. We got there but we were too early. There wasn't a soul about. We were sat on the benches and waited for people to come. It was still dark. We had a clock but it didn't work. We used to rely on the trams going by in the morning to know what time it was. We always knew The Civic Centre [bell] went every quarter of an hour. We were there for a while and then people started to turn up and we got on buses to the station and then on to Bournemouth.'*[6]*

As Mike Brown notes in *Evacuees of the Second World War* (2009), the Women's Voluntary Service or Girl Guides were often at railway stations, handing out refreshments. Most of the trains used for the evacuation were comprised of old rolling stock that were non-corridor compartments, without toilets. Luckily, they had windows, so boys, at least, were soon 'peeing out of the window.' In Petts Wood, Kent, children were taken off the trains to a specially-requisitioned field where trenches had been dug, over which pairs of wooden planks were placed side-by-side with a gap between, providing makeshift toilet facilities.

All evacuees had one thing in common: they had no idea where they were going. School teachers and volunteer helpers were given the responsibility for supervising the children but even they had no notion of their eventual destinations.

Billeting Officers had the unenviable job of finding places for those evacuated. Often, this entailed rounding up potential local hosts, or 'foster-parents' as they were known, and bringing them to village halls to view the children, lined up as if on parade. Many people opened their homes to these needy strangers, but not everyone did so willingly. Often there was not enough room for families travelling together and so they were split up.

Kathy's Avagah's sister Grace, aged 13 when she was evacuated from Dagenham, recalls, 'We set off for Lowestoft on the 'Golden Daffodil'. Mum, baby Teddy and Kathy went to Belton. I went to Bradwell with my sisters Ivy, ten and Dorothy, six. Meanwhile, Bobby and Ronnie were living in a converted train carriage in Bradwell.'[7]

The pretty, the strong and those on their own were chosen first.

Jack Flanagan was born in Liverpool in 1930. He and his sister, Mary, born in 1928, were evacuated by train to Winsford, Cheshire, thirty miles away.

'On arrival, we were all herded into the playground of one of the town's schools. Here we were chosen at random by the local people. There appeared to me to be no distribution system of any kind at all. I can only assume that my sister and I were the least attractive of the kids as we were some of the last chosen.'[8]

The scenes in the reception areas over the first few days of September were chaotic. In many, they would have been viewed as farcical if it were not for the fact that tired, homesick, hungry and frightened children were the victims of such fiascos. There were situations where children were sent to the wrong places and some who had got on the wrong trains. Villagers who were not expecting any evacuees suddenly received hundreds, while others who were expecting hundreds received none.

In Berkshire, the villagers of Hungerford, for example, were not supposed to receive any evacuees at all yet eight hundred of them turned up.[9] Amongst some of the rail confusions, children destined for Wales ended up in Leicester. Even where children were expected, the preparations for them were frequently inadequate. As Thelma Wolf remembered of her reception in Yarmouth:

'They didn't know what to do with us. There was no place to take us. There were no plans of where we were going. So, I suppose people in Yarmouth got this message that the boats were coming, and they opened up a school. I can remember what it looked like. It was just a bungalow building and usual iron railing round. They brought in trays of food, but it was all cold you know, sausage in red skins, apples and sausage rolls and white bread. That was when we arrived on the Friday. We still had the same on Saturday and Sunday. There was no hot food at all, it was pretty grim. The local people bought blankets for us.'[10]

All over the country there were children housed on makeshift beds of straw and sacks or whatever came to hand, while local billeting officers scoured the area for billets. Much of the accommodation that had been allocated to those evacuated under the government scheme had been already taken by private evacuees, many of whom had taken themselves into the countryside long before the official evacuation order was issued. Some accommodation had also been earmarked for servicemen. The lack of adequate housing and the conditions under which some evacuees were supposed to sleep resulted in a massive drift back to the cities within a mere two weeks. Some children in Scotland had been expected to live in outhouses, sleep on concrete floors and in rooms with no beds.[11] In England, a billeting officer in Oxfordshire reported in the first fortnight of evacuation that over fifty percent of mothers with young children had already returned to London because of inadequate accommodation.

It should also be pointed out that billeting officers were not always clear with regard to their duties. Most believed that their job was complete once they had placed their evacuees in suitable homes, when government officials believed their remit extended to supervising evacuees on a long-term basis.

Despite the dire shortage of available billets, there were still householders who flatly refused to comply with the compulsory billeting measures, and even chose imprisonment in preference to taking in evacuees. Middle, and upper-class householders, in particular, attempted to evade their responsibilities in this respect. This evasion did not go unnoticed. For example, in the *North Wales Chronicle* it was reported that:

> *Last Sunday evening (the day war was declared) I saw something I shall never forget. A little crowd of homeless schoolboys evacuated from Liverpool, sat huddled on the pavement in one of the most well to do areas of Bangor, outside the house of a married couple who refused to take them. The Billeting Officer had argued and begged. "You have seven empty rooms and no responsibilities. You are only taking one gown up. Can't you manage even two of these tired children?'" "No I can't," snapped the woman, and closed the door.*
>
> *While the Billeting Officer discussed what to do with the children, the garden gate opened and the 'lady' of the house emerged followed by her husband. They were going to church!*
>
> *They stepped daintily through the pathetic bundles, the haversacks and gas masks and the children watched them…saying nothing.[12]*

There were, of course, some reception areas such as Cambridgeshire, which were well organised, with members of the voluntary services on hand to offer the evacuees refreshment on arrival and basic first aid if required. But even the most organised of reception areas could be forgiven for lapses in efficiency when confronted with double or sometimes treble the number of expected evacuees. In extreme cases, children were billeted with prostitutes and abortionists and expected to sleep three or four to a bed widthways. For the evacuees themselves, however, the most humiliating experience on their arrival was the cattle market. Evacuees were literally herded together, some actually placed in cattle pens, while potential hosts looked them up and down and chose which children they would deign to accommodate. The process was both undignified and terrifying for the children concerned.

Doris Nicholson (née Cook) was nine when she was the only member of her family to be evacuated from Woodford, Ilford, Essex to Duddleston Road, Taunton, Somerset. She remembers being paraded in front of potential hosts:

> *'We went into the village hall and people came and looked at us. I wet my pants. I know I was nine but I was frightened. People looked us over. We didn't know a soul. It was horrible, really.'* [13]

Generally, host families chose those who could potentially be of use to them, in much the same way as animals were chosen at markets. In farming areas, teenage boys were usually the first to be picked, since they were sturdy enough to help out on the farms.

Above: Doris Nicholson was 9 when she was evacuated to Taunton, Somerset.

May Toone was evacuated from Croydon at the age of twelve with her younger sister. The two girls found themselves living on a large farm in Holsworthy, Devon. May remembers:

The farmer's wife was elderly and looked like a witch but was a lovely lady. I milked the cows by hand and fed the bull calves milk from a bucket. I learned a lot when the cows were brought to visit the bull! Interview, February 2017

Above: Jill Simmonds and her family on the beach at Barton-on-Sea, 1940. Left to Right: Jill aged 5, Michael aged 4, Tony aged 6, baby Roger aged 10 months, with their mother.

Just who would be prepared to house a mother with four children? We were the last family on the bus when it proceeded to head along a tree-lined drive to the most enormous house we had ever seen. It was 'Chewton Glen', which was to become our home for the next seven years. This lovely house now belonged to a very refined lady called Mrs Tinker. She and her staff must have been mortified by our invasion – almost as bad as Hitler, perhaps?! However, we soon grew on them and probably livened up what was, maybe, a dull way of life. We rarely saw the stately Mrs Tinker leave her exclusive quarters, except when she walked in the grounds with Topsy, her faithful Scottish terrier. Mrs Tinker was a tall, elegant lady, always dressed in black. The house has a famous literary link through the fact that Captain Frederick Marryat stayed there in the 1840s and gathered material for his successful novel 'Children of the New Forest'. Now the Elliotts were to become children of the New Forest.

Jill Simmonds, née Elliott, evacuated to New Milton just before her fifth birthday.

Left: The side elevation of Chewton Glen in 1940, when Jill Simmonds and her family were living there. Their bedrooms were in the attic. The main living area was above the steps.

Young boys were next in line since they would eventually grow to be farm hands. Girls were frequently chosen for their ability to help with domestic chores or their good looks. Enid Philpott and her sister Jean were evacuated to Milbourne Port. She remembers:

'We got to Milbourne Port and we were taken to the school and we got off the bus and the lady that was at the village hall said, 'Oh just come in,' and she beckoned us, and she said, 'you come here with me,' and she took us to the lady. Her name was Mrs Dyke and she wanted two little blonde girls with blue eyes and they didn't come more blonde or blue eyed than us.'[14]

Given this predictable pecking order then, expectant mothers and mothers with very small children stood very little chance of finding accommodation. When billets were found for these women and small children they were often in isolated localities.

Mrs Minton, who acted as host in the village of Mathen in Worcestershire declared that:

'We had a young mother with three children under the age of five years. On arrival the first question was, 'Where was the pub and the chip shop?' On being told that the pub was two miles away and the 'chippie' was the other side of the Malvern Hills five miles away, they nearly returned to Birmingham.'[15]

Meanwhile, Dee Williams was evacuated from Rotherhithe to Coolham, a village near Horsham in Kent, aged nine, with her five-year-old brother and her mother.

'We were taken to a farm. We were in an estate car driven by someone from the WVS (Women's Voluntary Service). She took us there and they weren't in. So, she took us back to the pub we'd been waiting in. They didn't have phones much in those days. She took others to their billets. A little while later, she took us back to the farm. They still weren't in. By now it was getting dark. When we came back to the pub again, she asked the landlord if we could stay the night. He said, "I don't do that but there is

Above: Dee Williams and her parents in happier times, at the beach before the war.

the barn out there. They can sleep in there." So, he gave us some straw palliases. It was a tin barn. It rained and the rain was bouncing off the roof. There was my poor mum, sitting there, crying her eyes out. My mother was never religious, but she said, "Now I know how Mary and Joseph felt, with no room in the inn!" Then, the next morning, Mr English, the farmer, came to collect us. When we got to his farm, his wife was standing on the doorstep with her arms folded. She said, "I tell you now, I don't want you but it's you or Land Girls. If we have Land Girls I have to wait on them. You can look after yourselves." That started my mother off again.'[16]

Video 10 Dee Williams:
Not welcome

Teachers also experienced accommodation problems and many were forced to tour the reception areas themselves in search of a billet. They had been told before their evacuation that their school identity would be maintained at all costs, but for most this proved to be impossible. School members were sometimes scattered over several villages and teachers had to cycle for miles to check on the wellbeing of their pupils. They were often re-evacuated, either because of accommodation problems or because they had been evacuated to the east coast and into the enemy firing line. In a few cases, schools were re-evacuated several times.

Some evacuees took re-evacuation in their stride but others were emotionally disturbed by the first move, let alone the second. Despite the fragile emotional state of many children, re-evacuation continued, some simply to make room for military personnel. For example, although Hereford City Council had forewarned the government that the city would not be able to accommodate both evacuees and military personnel, the city acquired five thousand evacuees. The approximate number of persons living in Hereford on 29 September 1939, along with the numbers they were supposed to incorporate, were as follows: The normal population amounted to 25,000 and an extra 5,000 had moved into the area. The surplus included evacuated children and voluntary evacuees, but it did not include troops. Councillors were informed by the government that accommodation was needed for a further 11,000 people. This number was made up of 750 troops, 1000 civil servants and 4250 munitions workers.[17]

Evacuees had been in Hereford less than two months before Mr C. Franklin of the Hereford Council Finance Committee wrote to the Ministry of Health demanding the immediate removal of eight hundred school children. Hereford had the unique distinction of being the only city in the country to be designated as a 'vulnerable reception' area and the logic of this decision was clearly questionable. Mrs S. Hodges, who had seconded the resolution stated, 'if there is no scheme made to take these children away, we should close our schools until there is one. We have no business to send children to school in a danger area.'[18] After a visit to the town from The First Commissioner of Works, the Rt. Honourable H. Ramsbottom OBE, MC, MP, accompanied by representatives of various interested government departments, arrangements were made to evacuate the children and by 27 August 1940 all evacuated school children had been removed from Hereford.[19]

In addition to the accommodation and location problems which led to re-evacuations, there was also a lack of basic supplies in the reception areas. Central government had promised abundant supplies of mattresses and blankets but these were not always forthcoming in the required number. When blankets did arrive, they were usually very thin and of poor quality. Health and education facilities in the rural areas could not even begin to cope under the strain of the unprecedented population growth. Sanitation was another problem. Scores of education authorities were forced to buy or lease extra land

Right: John Hammond, evacuated to Poole aged 11.

from local farmers in order to provide adequate sanitary facilities for extra school children. Schools were also forced to operate a 'shift system' whereby local children attended school in the mornings and evacuees in the afternoons or vice versa. John Hammond remembers just such an arrangement:

> *'I was in King Edward VI School in Southampton and we moved as a school and joined in, as separate schools, with Poole Grammar School. The arrangement was, we went in the morning, they went in the afternoon one week, then the next week we would swap over. That happened all the time.'*[20]

Where schools were very overcrowded, teachers took to educating their pupils in village halls, pubs or cinemas. Jill Simmonds, evacuated to Chewton Glen near New Milton with her mother and three siblings, remembers that the school she walked two miles to each day 'consisted of converted Army huts, used during the First World War. It was very, very basic.'[21]

Video 11 John Hammond: *Part-time school*

Councillors and the local inhabitants in reception areas became more and more disgruntled with the unfulfilled promises of Whitehall. Nor were the host families impressed with the billeting allowances. The weekly sum of ten shillings and six pence for the first child and eight shillings and six pence for subsequent children was not enough to cover board and lodging except in the case of very small

Video 12 Dee Williams, who became a noted novelist as an adult, moved several times and her schooling suffered as a result.

> *Yet another child was born into the family in 1943. Mother was rushed in the blackout, some 30 miles away to Shawford House, near Winchester, for her confinement. My brother, Robert is probably the only person to have 'Chewton Glen' noted on his Birth Certificate. The harassed staff probably had visions of Chewton Glen slowly turning into a kindergarten!*
>
> Jill Simmonds, née Elliott, evacuated to New Milton just before her fifth birthday.

children. There was no allowance made for clothes, shoes or or medical expenses, yet a good many of the evacuees were in dire need of all three of these. In particular, children from Newcastle, Liverpool and London were noted to be severely deficient in footwear and clothing. Hosts who found themselves with evacuees who wet the bed were, however, afforded an extra three shillings and six pence a

Video 13 Dee Williams: *Wetting the bed*

week in additional laundry allowances, an allowance fully exploited by some hosts not averse to lying about their evacuees. In the space of six months, the claims for extra laundry allowances more than trebled. These subsequently subsided after an official enquiry into the bed-wetting claims.

There were press reports which stated that expectant mothers were merely enjoying a holiday in the countryside and there were disputes over whether the evacuation or receiving authority should pay for their confinements. A few expectant mothers found themselves unceremoniously bundled on to the next available train heading for London so that the reception area could avoid the cost of confinement.

Likewise, authorities bickered over the funeral expenses of evacuees who died in their reception areas. After much deliberation, the Ministry of Health stated that the government were prepared to pay for the funerals of evacuees, provided that the funeral took place in the reception area. They would pay the rail fares of grieving relatives but they would not pay to transport the body back to home territory. This decision inevitably led to more heartbreak for some families.

Not all problems associated with billeting could be attributed to a lack of money, essential supplies and services. Even before the evacuees had set foot in the reception areas, rumours had spread through urban and rural communities of the sick, mal-nourished, verminous, bad-mannered and dirty urchins who normally inhabited the big cities. Such was the belief in these rumours that many children were subjected to vigorous scrubbing and disinfecting baths. In North Wales, the hospitable inhabitants adopted extreme measures to ensure the cleanliness of their evacuees. When they arrived in their allotted billets, evacuees were forced to strip, often in front of host family members, get into a hot tin bath, which had been laced with Dettol, and have their heads completely shaved. In some instances, Liverpool children even had their clothes burned as an extra precaution against lice. This horrific experience ensured that all evacuees in the community stood out from the local children.[22]

Evacuees were consistently blamed for introducing scabies, headlice and infectious diseases into the countryside, despite the fact that all these conditions already existed in the reception areas before their arrival. Not only were they deemed to be responsible for all infestations, they were also accused of vandalism, petty thieving and arson. Exaggerated tales were usually propagated by middle-class women who stated that evacuees did not know how to use cutlery, were not house trained when it came to toilet habits and did not know how to wash or clean their teeth. The evacuees were equally confused. Many children found themselves working hard, particularly those sent to farms. Raymond Banks, evacuated at the age of eleven from Southampton to New Milton in Hampshire with his younger brother Kenneth, remembers getting up at five o'clock to bring the cows home. He had to get them across a bridge over a railway line before he could go off to school.[23]

The level of poverty amongst the evacuees shocked the nation, including those in Whitehall; but there were also those who had left middle-class homes who were equally shocked by their working-class billets. After a few chaotic months, and the emergence of hostile relationships in the reception areas, it became increasingly clear that the government evacuation scheme was failing dismally. Reception areas had been stretched to the limits of their endurance.

The expected aerial bombardment of major cities had not occurred. The 'Phoney War', effectively the 'calm before the storm' had prompted a gradual return to the cities. Over 80 percent of evacuees had returned home by January 1940. As Peter Mooney, aged eleven when he was evacuated, simply states, 'We returned to Southampton because the raids hadn't materialised like they thought they were going to.'[24]

The government were, nonetheless, committed to evacuation as part of their civil defence strategy and, at a special conference on evacuation on 22 January 1940, the Home Secretary sought to reassure future potential hosts of government support:

Above: Peter Mooney and siblings. Peter was evacuated from Southampton, aged 11.

'Everything must be done to ensure that in future movement the burden falling on householders was relieved as far as possible, and that the physical condition of the children did not give rise to difficulties. There must also be further arrangements for education. While the position in the reception and neutral areas was not unsatisfactory, the position in the evacuation areas was far from satisfactory, and every effort would have to be made to release school buildings which had been diverted to civil defence purposes.'[25]

Video 14 George Bert: *School*

This statement showed how out of touch the Home Secretary was. Education was not fine in the reception and neutral areas, as any teacher trying to cope with overcrowding and the shift system could have told him. The government was at an impasse: ministers did not want to reopen schools in evacuation areas for fear that evacuees would be encouraged by this action to return to the cities. However, if those same schools remained closed, thousands of children would go without education. Furthermore, although ministers were genuinely shocked by the level of evacuee poverty, the blame was laid firmly at the door of working-class parents. Members of the working-class were labelled as idle or mentally defective. The Women's Group on Public Welfare concluded:

The effect of evacuation was to flood the dark places with light and bring home to the national consciousness that the 'submerged tenth' described by Charles Booth still exists in our towns like a hidden sore, poor, dirty and crude in its habits, and an intolerable and degrading burden to decent people forced by poverty to neighbour with it. Within this group are the 'problem' families, always on the edge of pauperism and crime, riddled with mental and physical defects, in and out of the Courts for child neglect, a menace to the community of which the gravity is out of all proportion to their numbers.[26]

Video 15 Dee Williams: *Life in Rotherhithe*

The patronising attitudes of middle-class women who enjoyed playing the role of 'Lady Bountiful' throughout the war did little to help the root cause of evacuee poverty. The conference on evacuation studiously overlooked the poverty issues and likewise failed to tackle any of the problems which were associated with human relationships and social dislocation.

Ministers had the opportunity to learn from the experiences of Operation Pied Piper, but very few lessons were taken on board. As school children embarked on the next wave of evacuation, most of the problems in the reception areas remained unresolved.

Video 16 George Bert: *Life in Greenwich*

Video 17 Ray Banks: *Posh houses vs ordinary houses*

Endnotes

1 *Hansard Parliamentary Debates House of Commons 5th Series*, 14 September 1939, cols 824, 884

2 Interview with Jean Banks, 2016

3 Family account written by Kathy Avagah, undated

4 Oral history interview Cambridge University evacuation project, Thelma Wolfe, 1999. See also extracts from the internally printed gazettes of the Waltham Forest History Workshop.

5 Interview with Ken Oakley, 2016

6 Interview with John Bowen, 2016

7 Family account written by Kathy Avagah, undated

8 Interview with Jack Flanagan, 2016

9 Parsons, M., *I'll Take That One* (Peterborough, 1998), p.58

10 Oral history interview Cambridge University evacuation project, Thelma Wolfe, 1999

11 *Hansard Parliamentary Debates House of Commons, 5th Series* 14 September 1939, col 875

12 Article entitled 'Something I Shall Never Forget' *North Wales Chronicle* 8 September 1939, quoted in M. Parsons I'll Take That One (1998), p. 126

13 Interview with Doris Nicholson, 2016

14 Interview with Enid Philpott, 2016

15 Hereford County Record Office ref BK13/1/45 the recollections of Gladys Minton

16 Interview with Dee Williams, 2016

17 Herefordshire County Record Office: Minutes of the Air Raid Precautions Committee 1938-1939, figures submitted on 11 November 1939, p. 986.

18 'A Vulnerable Reception Area' Journal of Education vol LXXIV no 1921 3 November 1939, p. 374.

19 Herefordshire County Record Office: Minutes of the Air Raid Precautions Committee 1938 – 1939, statement made on 11 June 1940, p. 229

20 Interview with John Hammond, 2016

21 Interview with Jill Simmonds, 2016

22 Parsons, M., *I'll Take That One* (1998) p. 14

23 Interview with Raymond Banks, 2016

24 Interview with Peter Mooney, 2016

25 Official Conference on Evacuation National Archives ED/136/125

26 Women's Group on Public Welfare, *Our Towns, A Close-Up* (London, 1943) p. xiii. Quoted in J. Macnicol, 'The Evacuation of School Children' H. Smith, (eds) *War and Social Change* (Manchester, 1986) p.24

Above: A recruiting poster urging women to become ARP wardens.

Chapter 2
Evacuation 1940

*'I was not really happy about being sent off
to live with strangers in another town.'*

Terence Randall, evacuated from Southampton, aged 8

In April 1940, the British were defeated in their Norwegian campaign and on 10 May Neville Chamberlain resigned his position as British Prime Minister. His handling of political events both before the war and during the first few months of conflict had prompted severe criticism. The loss of political and public confidence in Chamberlain resulted in the formation of a coalition government headed by Winston Churchill, on May 10th. On the same day the Germans invaded the Netherlands, Belgium and Luxembourg. Two days later, they invaded France prompting the Dunkirk retreat. Then, on September 7th, the blitz began. The German Luftwaffe subjected major British cities and ports to unremitting waves of aerial bombardment. More than fifty percent of all British civilian casualties (over 80,000) were sustained between September 1940 and May 1941.[1]

Video 18 John Hammond:
Dog fights

In the summer of 1940, reception areas across Britain prepared for another onslaught of evacuees. In the same year, a London correspondent for the *New York Herald* pronounced: 'Hitler is doing what centuries of English history have not accomplished – he is breaking down the class structure of England.'[2] In fact, evacuation did more to reinforce those boundaries by confirming the worst nightmares of the middle class. In an attempt to unite against a common enemy, a 'camaraderie' between the classes was manufactured, often for

Video 19 Jean & Ray Banks:
The bombing of Southampton

propaganda purposes. 'But for all the feeling that Britain was a united nation, this was in many ways just that: a mood, a feeling, a vision, but no more.'[3]

39

Inside this vision, evacuees provided an uncomfortable reminder of a supposedly bygone age. No longer the deserving or undeserving poor of Victorian Britain, they were, nonetheless, a very visible poor. A proportion of host families tried to help those who were, in many cases, less fortunate than themselves, but there were also those who were more preoccupied with protecting their own interests. In the reception areas, shortcomings in health and education services were blamed on evacuees in much the same way as rising crime levels. The American government issued their troops with *Welcome to Britain*, a booklet designed to acquaint American servicemen with British life and customs. This stated a Briton, 'is the most law-abiding citizen in the world, because the British system of justice is just about the best there is. There are fewer murders, robberies and burglaries in the whole of Great Britain in a year than in a single large American city.'[4] Regardless of what the Americans thought, nationally crime in Britain rose to fifty-seven percent from its pre-war level.[5] Local children were viewed as paragons of virtue while evacuees were stereotyped as disease-ridden vagabonds. The second and third waves of evacuation did little to change these views. In fact, the notion of the 'dirty evacuee' became one of the most pervasive stereotypes of the war, despite tangible evidence to the contrary. Billeting problems were compounded as more evacuees were ushered into the countryside, and child health and education continued to suffer.

> *The kitchen garden was a sight to be seen and we soon learned to 'scrump', particularly the cordon pears from the surrounding wall. It was my job to scale a plank and pick the pears, whilst my eldest brother, Tony, 'kept watch.' Needless to say, he was the first one to scarper when Mr Weaver, the Head Gardener, appeared on the scene, leaving me to face the music!*
> Jill Simmonds, née Elliott, evacuated to New Milton just before her fifth birthday.

Inevitably, the drive for compulsory evacuation surfaced once again, following the British retreat from Dunkirk and the possibility of an imminent invasion. According to Labour's Colonel Wedgewood, the prospect of another evacuation failure would have dire consequences on the fighting forces:

> *'Imagine for one moment that this country is invaded. Every man worth his salt will be engaged either in the field, or in some munitions factory far from his family. All the time they will be anxious about what is happening to their wives, children and parents. I do not blame the Belgians for surrendering, and I should not blame the French if they*

surrendered. What is an army to do when they see those dismal columns of helpless women and children and when they think that their own women and children may be among such crowds, being mercilessly machine-gunned while starving and dropping and dying of exhaustion by the roadside? If that is the fate of womankind, you cannot expect an army to fight. Therefore, this problem of evacuation is a very real one and does not apply solely to children. It applies to all useless mouths in every country which is meeting this form of gangster warfare.'[6]

Colonel Wedgewood was one of the first speakers in the House of Commons to openly refer to sections of the population as 'useless mouths'. This term became an increasingly popular way of describing children from 1940 onwards. But Wedgewood's assessment of the situation was fundamentally flawed. The majority of women could not be classed in the 'useless mouths' category since most were actually working in munitions factories, manning the hospitals and first aid stations, cultivating the land and assisting the fighting forces. Neither did the government view women as being in this category. Indeed, the need to keep women working in these essential services was the prime motive for shifting their children to the reception areas.

Wedgewood did have a valid point in that the morale of all members of the fighting forces would suffer if the government did not appear to be doing something in order to protect their families. But evacuees in the reception areas were frequently viewed as unwelcome lodgers. Jack Flanagan, born in 1930, was evacuated from Liverpool to Winsford, Cheshire, with his sister, Mary, born in 1928. He remembers:

'We went to live with a Mrs Hulse but regretfully they were not happy times. There was little warmth in the family. My sister and I were compelled to go to church three times a day on a Sunday: coming from a non-church-

Video 20 George Burt:
The woman from hell

going family, like ours, it was an unpleasant ordeal. I remember the daughter of the family most certainly resented us being there. My sister and I were required to sleep together and being a very nervous little lad, I frequently wet the bed. Because of this, we were parted. This came hard to me as I had never been parted from my sister Mary, to whom I was very close.[7]

Eight thousand of the children who had registered for evacuation in 1940 remained in London because local authorities were unable to find billets for them.[8]

Above: A wartime propaganda poster urging mothers to evacuate their children to safety.

'No one seemed interested in my brother and I and we were the last two children left. So the WVS lady said we were to go with her, as luck would have it, she turned out to be 'tlady of the manor.' When everyone else had gone we were told to go to the car to wait for her, a Jaguar, never had we been in such luxury transport. So we were driven down the road to West Stafford House.

The butler opened the door to us and we were ushered into the servants' quarters to meet the rest of the household. We could not believe our luck finding ourselves in such grandiose surroundings.

After school we would wander and explore the vast estate of Stafford House. The chores we had to do were feeding the poultry and going to the kitchen garden, which was the other end of the village. We pushed a very large trailer to collect all the fallen apples, then pushed it back to feed to the pigs on the estate. We would help feed the pheasants in the spinney with corn, so the owner Mr Redfern could organise a 'shoot' later in the year. For our work, if that is what you could call it, we received 2/6 a week, a small fortune to us in those days.'

Dennis Edward Carrett

Dennis saw in the paper that West Stafford House had been bought by Mr Julian Fellows, so he wrote to him with information about his years there. Mr Fellows wrote by return of post wanting lots of information about staff etc. They had continuing letters to and forth and he and I were invited to Stafford House, to tour the house and to have lunch with him, his wife and other guests. He, Mr Fellows, was delighted to know there had been a kitchen garden, 'as the best lawyers in London' could not find any trace of one.

Mr Fellows became Lord Fellows after Downton Abbey was made into an award-winning television programme. Dennis always felt pride that the information he gave might have helped with the programme.

Patricia Carrett

The general public began to demonstrate widespread dissatisfaction with evacuation and the numerous incidences of bureaucratic incompetence. Both parents and host families alike had lost faith in government assurances. In an effort to combat this problem, the government embarked on a propaganda campaign to 'enlighten' the public. The campaign adopted a two-pronged approach. First, propaganda tried to persuade parents to evacuate their children as a matter of urgency if they had not already done so, and not to collect those children who were already in the reception areas. Secondly, the campaign appealed to the 'national duty' of potential and existing hosts in the reception areas, in the hope of acquiring more billets for further evacuees. To ease the accommodation problem, the government also opened thirty-one camp schools and attempted to utilise unused mansions.

As the government tried to portray evacuation as a positive by-product of war, their propaganda campaigns met with some difficulties. Various government departments tried to gain information which would support the view that children were happier, safer and healthier in the county. A memo from the Board of Education to school inspectors in February 1940 explained:

> *'What we should like to have is not a report of a formal statistical nature but rather the kind of story which reveals the span and attitude of children, teachers and foster parents and so on, and which illustrates some of the social and educational effects of bringing children from towns and into different surroundings'*[9]

There was, however, no evidence to suggest that children were happier or healthier in the reception areas. It was even debatable whether children were safer, since many of the rural schools had no air raid shelters whatsoever. Ray Banks remembers the bombing of New Milton in Hampshire as a twelve-year-old, when he and his companion became targets for enemy gunfire:

> *'We heard an aircraft in the distance. Pete, the chap I was with, said, "that sounds like a German, Ray, doesn't it?"*
>
> *"Yeah."* [Ray impersonates the sound – whum, whum, whum.]
>
> *'We looked up, towards New Milton. He said, "Cor, it's not far above the roofs!"*
>
> *'We watched this plane coming towards us. As we were watching, we saw the doors come open and a string of bombs came out. Then, the next thing, an explosion and all the dust and muck and all up in the air. He hit a builder's merchant and the adjoining buildings.*
>
> *'We were so frightened. Pete said, "Come on, Ray, quick, get out of the way." As we started to run towards the hedge, we heard gunfire coming from the plane, which frightened us even more. When that started, we jumped into this hedge and at the back of the hedge there was a ditch to take off surface water from the fields. We landed up in there, all covered in mud and stinging nettles and thistles and goodness knows what. We were in there, we looked up and the German bomber was*

Above: This propaganda poster urges those in the reception areas to accept the wave of evacuees sent to them. Whether through wartime stringences or subtle emotion the poster uses the same pair of children shown on the previous poster.

Above: With thousands of evacuees returning to their homes, this wartime poster urges mothers to leave their children in the relative safety of the evacuation areas.

going across and you could see the chappy in the front part of the aeroplane and a chappy with a gun. [...] We watched as far as we could. The next thing we could hear aircraft – Spitfires and Hurricanes – as it got further away. There was gunfire, rapid gunfire, coming from the aircraft. They shot the big German aircraft down in the Solent. We were so shaken up, we stayed there for quite some time. It was very uncomfortable but we stayed there as long as we could.'[10]

Video 21 Ray Banks:
Under attack in New Milton

Propaganda posters were unable to state with any degree of authority that the countryside was more beneficial for children than city life. Consequently, posters exploited parental emotions of guilt and fear. One of the most famous posters showed mothers blissfully sharing a rural picnic with their children with the sinister figure of Hitler hiding behind a tree whispering 'Take them back.' A later propaganda film entitled *Westward Ho* included emotional appeals to British mothers from Belgium and French mothers who stated that: it was now too late for them to evacuate their children but not too late for British mothers. The film also included the views of ordinary British soldiers who claimed that 'if we know our children our safe we will fight better.'[11]

Officials also attempted to defend Operation Pied Piper, and complained that adult evacuees had discussed the facilities provided in this earlier evacuation scheme as though they were weak features of a holiday tour rather than an organised plan to safeguard their wellbeing. Another propaganda film entitled *Living with Strangers* highlighted the difficulties of billeting officers, host families and evacuees. The film appealed for a greater spirit of co-operation, tolerance and understanding in the reception areas.[12] The quantity and quality of evacuation propaganda, which emanated from the Ministry of Information, represented an urgent attempt to gain public support for the 'dispersal' policy. But government policy was contradictory. Although the propaganda tried to convince parents to leave their children in the country, at the same time the government insisted that all parents should pay billeting allowances. Since many parents could not afford these payments, the policy clearly undermined any attempt to keep children in reception areas. It is also difficult to assess the impact of propaganda. Certainly the second and third waves of evacuation were more successful in terms of the actual numbers of evacuees who stayed in the reception areas. Later evacuation waves, however, were genuine flights from aerial bombardment rather than precautions. New reluctance on the part of evacuees to leave reception areas owed more to enemy action than to government propaganda.

Officials were, nonetheless, anxious to avoid a repeat of Operation Pied Piper. As a consequence, subsequent evacuations took place as a genuine response to imminent danger and most children underwent medical inspections before they left their evacuation areas. Travel arrangements, however, were just as appalling. Mrs Hellier, a teacher from Stoke Newington, described her experience as follows:

> My party went by train to Melksham, a lovely little country town in Wiltshire. It was a very hot day and just before the train started helpers came along with mugs and buckets of water for the children to have a drink. Alas my party did not get any because we had been shown into the guard's van. We could not sit down on the journey as the floor was dirty and smelled of fish. It was a long uncomfortable journey, but the children endured it with stoicism.[13]

Another teacher recalled how she and her colleagues hunted the streets of 'neutral zone' Plymouth for children the day before their emergency evacuation.

> During that time the blitz was extremely bad particularly where my children lived. On the Sunday night my friend and I went amongst all the blitzed houses where the children had been in their shelters night after night, telling them to meet us at the station the next day. We got on the train on the Monday and landed in Tambourine. We were all turfed out and the children were taken to the school to be examined for dirty heads and impetigo. Farmers came and picked the big boys and girls to work on the farm but we were not billeted until nighttime. We eventually ended up in a village called Coverack but we were not always safe. One day my friend Winnie was walking down to the beach with her party of school children and suddenly a plane appeared over the top of the houses. She said she could see him as plainly as anything, and he dropped four bombs across the village. Several people were killed. The telephone wires and everything came down over our children. But they had been used to ducking for many moons. The plane then proceeded to machine gun people on the beach. Our children were alright but it was a worrying time.[14]

Reception areas were generally more organised second time around, but overcrowding remained a problem. The blitz of major cities by the German Luftwaffe had prompted a change of attitude in some receptions, and many hosts exhibited a genuine sympathy for the plight of evacuees.

Nevertheless, evacuees were still viewed by many as unwelcome lodgers; and this was not merely a case of middle-class hosts rejecting working-class evacuees since hostility was extended equally to middle-class adults and children. A producer working at the BBC and evacuated to Evesham stated:

My billet is vile. Its owners seem to regard one rather as if one was... likely to steal the family silver and ravish the daughter as opposed to hoping for bed and breakfast. I fancy, too, that one's inevitably irregular hours of going and coming have raised doubts in their minds about one's morals. [15]

Video 22 George Burt: Life was good

The growing numbers of BBC employees who were required to speak several languages caused further consternation in reception areas. The local population treated all these employees with a high degree of suspicion and those who spoke German were frequently reported to the police on suspicion of being enemy spies. An Austrian gentleman called Martin Esslin who worked as a monitor for the German section claimed, 'it would need a very great writer like George Eliot to describe the social and sexual revolution that was caused. Almost every possible nationality was here. Arabs, Russian counts, French gigolos... some of these foreigners were great seducers. The impact on Evesham was absolutely hilarious but tragic, too, in some ways.' [16]

Resentment in most cases can be seen as a knee jerk reaction by settled communities who were suddenly required to accommodate strangers en masse. There were hosts who resented the cost of feeding evacuees for instance, whereas others simply did not want to be responsible for children who were not their own.

My brother Victor and I had our first taste of being evacuated, to Newbury, dreadful place. We ran away and the man came after us on his motorbike and took us back. Mum and Dad came to visit with Dad's boss in his car. They found my brother and I sent outside to eat bread and dripping while the adults were inside having a good meal. We were taken home.

Dennis Edward Carrett – evacuated from Southampton with his brother Victor to Newbury, 1939

There were also those with legitimate difficulties, such as hosts who were old, ill or disabled encumbered with energetic young children because of the compulsory billeting system. Consequently, billeting officers were inundated with requests to re-house 'problem' evacuees. In some cases, hosts were able to get rid of their unwanted evacuees by claiming that they were badly behaved or suffered from constant bedwetting. These children were then taken to hostels and institutionalised. In Coverack, the local hospital for eneuretics was nicknamed the 'Hostile'.

Video 23 Dee Williams: *The countryside, an exciting place*

Overcrowding was not the only problem as both children and adults came to grips with new experiences and old prejudices. City children were forced for the first time to come to terms with the pace and style of country life, along with unfamiliar customs and habits. This adjustment was made all the more difficult by widely held, and ill-informed, notions of lifestyles of city children. A report in the Dorset press claimed that, since their arrival in Dorset, London children were 'learning to walk again' as if they had never walked before in their lives.[17] Yet city children were no strangers to exercise. They had in fact walked to the local schools, and played physical games in the streets every evening long before evacuation. While it was true that evacuees did not know how to operate farm machinery and oil lamps, and were strangers to collecting water from the pump, they were children just the same. Those who were not suffering from homesickness were just curious, playful and eager to explore their new surroundings.

Video 24 Jean and Ray Banks: *Food*

The chaotic mixing of children from different social strata did not result in an unprecedented culture clash, because working-class children were,

---

In Cerne Abbas you had a bakers' shop and a grocery shop. I used to love going round the blacksmith. He used to let me pump the bellows. The first time I saw him shoe a horse, I love horses, I said "You're burning him!" All the smoke rising. "No, I'm not. He don't feel it." I used to go around there every day. I loved that.
Roy Webb, evacuated from Southampton to Cerne Abbas, aged six

The little town, Bruton, Somerset, had hardly changed and on the surface at least appears to be the bastion of moral virtue, that is until an American army regiment descended on the town to rest a few weeks prior to going over on D-Day. To promote "Anglo-American" relations many of the ladies of Bruton were only too willing to take part in the goodwill campaign. A lady a few doors away was a very willing participant. The American boys showed their appreciation by rewarding her by bringing her huge tins, ten inches by ten inches, of food rations. The trouble for the lady in question was her husband was about to come home on leave at the weekend and she had all these huge ration tins in the house still. She was desperate. In her distress she called me over to her house and said if she gave me half a crown would I get rid of the tins after dark. So getting out (my) two wheeled box truck I would use for collecting rabbit food, I loaded up the truck and under the cloak of a very black winter night, I pushed the incriminating evidence up the solitary lane to a point some two miles out. I found a deep ditch and to the very call of the distant owls I buried all the tins deep into the undergrowth, much to the profound relief of everyone. When the American lads left for D-Day many never to return, the little town made a very brave but vain attempt to return to former times, but no it was not to be and people with long and often malicious memories still wagged their fingers for many years to come.

Jack Flanagan – *Tears Twice Over*

The lovely 1940 summer continued and we went to pick blackberries. I can remember being very upset when I dropped my jam jar and it disappeared down a rabbit hole.

John Virgo – evacuated from Southampton to Higher Loop Farm, Lytchett Matravers, Dorset, June 1940

more often than not, billeted with working class families. The middle classes were adept at shirking their responsibilities in this respect.

There were, however, some working-class evacuees who found themselves conforming to middle-class lifestyles. Most complained bitterly about the rigid meal times, stilted table manners, frequent baths and polite conversation.

I've heard this so often said as with most of the evacuees from the cities we developed a deep love and appreciation of the countryside. To me it was a sublime and spiritual revelation to see, hear and experience the beauty of the fields and woods around me, and at the age of 84, this deep and lasting joy remains undiminished and is with me still. In a way the countryside was our playground. No one seemed to worry about trespass, we wandered everywhere. One little instance I will remember is when one of the village lads and I visited an old abandoned and deserted cowshed and buried under the earth floor I found thirty-two half-pound packets of high explosives. These I laid neatly in a row on one of the roof trusses. When the police were informed the whole area was cordoned off. The mystery was never explained.

Jack Flanagan – *Tears Twice Over*

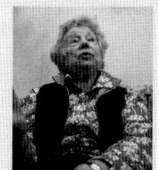 

Video 25 Janet Hammond: *A very happy time*

Video 26 George Bert: *Up to mischief – scent making*

Contemporary surveys found that London children badly missed the close-knit communities of the East End. Those who were billeted in Oxford protested that the place was 'full of forbidding old ladies' who hovered behind curtains, waiting to report children who played in the street too noisily. One young girl claimed: 'I cannot do as I like in the house. I must also come in when I am told and sit down and eat my meal properly and not run out into the street with a slice of bread in my hand.'

Middle-class evacuees were also confronted with new experiences. Those who had been evacuated from Kent to the Welsh valleys expressed shock when the Welsh miners came home at night and proceeded to strip off in the living rooms and plunge into tin baths. They were equally appalled at having to walk outside to use the toilet. A few children were not shown how to use the toilets.

'It was pitch dark inside and feeling around for the lav, all I could feel was a wooden bowl about three foot wide with a flat wooden top. By that time I couldn't hold out much longer, I did my business on top of the box. It was found later what I had done, much to my shame. How was I to know

you were supposed to lift the great heavy lid, where there was a second board with a round hole in it? I was told, the lid was there to keep the rats out, which didn't help my confidence one bit.'[18]

George Burt remembers his first thoughts on his new home:

'One thing I found very strange was that there was no gas, electricity or water connected to the house and certainly no flush toilet, which was situated outside and consisted of a seat with bucket under and torn-up newspapers

Video 27 George Bert: Fishing

when required. All lighting was by paraffin lamps and water had to be fetched from a communal tap at the end of the road by bucket. This became one of my jobs. I found it all rather surprising.'[19]

Outside toilets were also responsible for some of the cases of bedwetting. City children, used to indoor facilities, were understandably reluctant to go outside in the dark into an unfamiliar environment. They also claimed that the countryside at night was full of strange animal noises.

> **Terrence Randall remembers waking in Parkstone on his first morning as an evacuee from Northam, Southampton:**
>
> *I remember waking the next morning to the sound of a Westminster chimes clock striking the hour of NINE! I must have just died, small wonder when one realises what an eight-year-old had gone through in the previous 24 hours. We then discovered the joys of a bathroom, with hot water – not just running water – and 'one of the seven wonders of the world' – an indoor loo!*

John Hammond was born in Shirley, Southampton and attended a local preparatory school before going to King Edward VI School, an educational establishment with a history stretching back more than 465 years. John was eleven when the school was evacuated to Poole Grammar School.

Video 28 John Hammond: Duodecimals

'I stayed with the same family for five years. I was fortunate. I was put with a reasonable family. They were working-class but he was a very nice man, a lumberjack and a member of the Parkstone Conservative Club where he would meet his friends and have a drink. He liked to play

draughts and taught me that. He taught me duodecimals – working out cubic capacity of timber. You work in 12s instead of 10s. I used to be very adept at this. He got bonused on the quantity of timber he cut down and squared off. He was a very nice, gentle type of man. His wife did all the right things but was not so gentle. I hate to say it but she was a little bit lower class, coarser. Had no interest in anything cultural at all, reading, music.'[20]

The children who adapted to their surroundings, however, were quick to run rings around their town and country cousins. Teachers frequently referred to these children as belonging to the 'wide awake club'. Two young boys who had been evacuated from Manchester to Blackpool for instance, quickly realised that the trays of tea which were sold from the promenade kiosks were sold on condition that the customers left a shilling deposit for their teapot. The boys then patronised Woolworth's where they bought several teapots for nine and a half pennies each and took them back to the kiosks at regular intervals to claim the shilling teapot deposits. They duly pocketed the difference.[21]

The minds of city children proved to be quicker and sharper than those of country children. George Burt remembers how he thought it would be a good idea to make fireworks. His fellow nine-year-old friends agreed with him:

Video 29 George Bert: *Up to mischief – fireworks*

One day, we decided to make some homemade fireworks from some sulphur and saltpeter, which we were able to purchase quite easily from the local ironmonger. The mixture was very volatile and when lit made an awful smell. It was not a good idea to get any of the burning material on your hands or you would end up with a nasty burn. However, we never thought of that! We were not very popular when the fireworks were lit – the smell was terrible![22]

The influx of these quick-witted children into rural schools provided an obvious boost in the classroom. It was often not long before country-based teachers began to use city children to speed up the progress of their own pupils. This fundamental difference in child behaviour was even noticeable when evacuee children watched cinema shows.

Unlike the usual children's matinees they were very quiet, attentive and generally well behaved. There were some comments on the amount of noise cheering, booing, and so forth; this would be due to the contrast between evacuees from large towns where they think quickly, express

*themselves sharply and are confirmed cinema goers, and the local
country-born children whose reactions are much slower and less vocal.[23]*
The country-born children, however, did have the upper hand when it came to
dealing with the practicalities of rural life. They also revelled in the knowledge
that their city counterparts had not known on their arrival that apples grew on
trees and milk came from a cow.

Contemporary surveys and reports offer conflicting views of the ongoing
social upheaval. According to the National Federation of Women's Institutes,
working-class children who found themselves in middle-class homes were
extremely lucky, since these children could now begin the process of learning
how to be civilised. This process, they argued, would bring about an
improvement in the manners, health and attitude of children. They went on to
extol the virtues of middle-class family life, and claimed there had been few
incidences of homesickness amongst evacuees placed in these ideal homes. The
report to the Fabian Society and surveys conducted in Oxford and Cambridge
revealed a different story. Unlike the patronising sentiments expressed by
middle-class women, they cited frequent incidences of homesickness. Adult
evacuees who were living in middle-class homes complained of a general feeling
of humiliation, while children usually expressed a wish to return home. These
surveys were unique in that they included the views of children alongside that
of parents, hosts, teachers, welfare workers and billeting officers. Contrary to
popular middle-class opinion, they also confirmed the strength of working-class
ties in the face of enforced separation.

The fact that no-one knew how long the evacuees would need to stay within
individual host communities contributed to their status as unwelcome lodgers.
Furthermore, the prospect that evacuees might actually maintain a long-term
presence in the reception areas was a matter of great concern for specific
political and religious groups. Members of the Welsh Nationalist Party, for
example, were horrified by the thought that the Welsh-speaking population
would be diluted by English-speaking children. Catholic priests in Liverpool
were convinced that children evacuated to Protestant and Methodist Wales were
in severe moral danger. One Liverpool priest even advised parents to bring their
evacuated children back to Liverpool despite the serious risk of bombing,
because in his view the German bombs posed a lesser threat than that of moral
and spiritual corruption.[24] In the event, the fears expressed by the Welsh
Nationalists were unfounded. English children who were evacuated to Wales
not only managed to master the Welsh language, but also competed in the local
Eisteddfods.

The religious problems were more difficult to confront. Many Catholic children were forced to walk several miles every Sunday morning in order to attend mass and were forbidden to go near any form of Methodist or Protestant church. Religious intolerance was not merely a Catholic, Protestant and Methodist problem. There was also entrenched hostility between the Welsh Protestant and Welsh Methodist religion. For some evacuees, the memories of these entrenched religious differences all but swamped other recollections. Arthur Jones, who was evacuated at the age of five years to Meliden, in North Wales remembered:

'Opposite the Welsh Church there was a Methodist Church and my impression of this was "you must keep away from there". It was as though it was a witches place. When I returned to Liverpool I was in my teens and the church I found most acceptable was in fact the Methodist Church. I remember, to me it's so vivid the way everybody used to treat the Methodist Church, even walk on the opposite side of the road to it. I was really brainwashed over that.' [25]

George Burt, evacuated aged seven to a village just outside Whitland, was billeted with Mr and Mrs Reynolds. He remembers going to church for another reason:

'On Sunday morning, I attended the Church of Wales, in the afternoon Sunday School, then in the evening Mrs Reynolds took me to the baptist church in Whitland where the preacher spoke only Welsh and all his sermons were of the fire and brimstone type, which really scared me. When he said The Lord's Prayer, he spoke in Welsh, shouting his head off. I was really, really scared of him'. [26]

Video 30 George Bert: *Sunday school*

Ignorance of certain religions also posed problems, particularly for Jewish evacuees. For instance, hosts in some areas labelled Jewish children as ungrateful because they refused to tuck into meals which consisted of pork sausages and bacon. Other hosts even went so far as to blame them for the outbreak of war. As a young girl, Claire Rayner's Jewishness was discovered. and one farmer informed her that: 'We're fighting this war for the likes of you and I'm buggered if I can see why we're bothering.' [27]

Religious concerns gathered momentum and the Protestant churches of England and Wales embarked on what was called a New Crusade. A leading article in *The Times* of 17 February 1940 began the crusade by whipping up religious fervour and generating a public fear of moral degeneration. A series of ill-informed and ridiculous statements claimed that children were at risk of serious moral decline unless their education was solely based on Christian teaching. *The Times* stayed on this religious bandwagon for a year and in February 1941 reminded its readership of how often it had campaigned for a 'real Christian educational system for the children of a Christian land.'[28] Eventually, Lambeth Palace issued a statement which argued for the need for compulsory Christian teaching in all schools. There were also suggestions that teachers, members of local education authorities and school managers should all be 'tested' on their religious convictions. The whole crusade movement appeared to be accompanied by a sense of urgency, as an article in the *Education Journal* claimed: 'The public is now looking for such reforms but will become apathetic again if action be too long delayed: and each year a further batch of semi-pagan children passes from school life into citizenship.'[29] There were, however, a number of teachers who recognized the absurdity of the New Crusade. With references to the suggestion that teachers be tested on their convictions and morals, a man called Frank Roscoe wrote: 'in these grey days the magnificent silliness of the suggestion gives welcome excuse for mirth.'[30]

A headmaster from Cambridge Heath was equally scathing in a letter to the editor of *Education Journal*:

Sir,- I am one of those (there must be many) who are grateful to your journal for the statesmanlike attitude you have taken in this delicate and difficult matter of religious teaching. Those of us who do not see eye to eye with the ecclesiastical hierarchy are beginning to wonder whether we are to be examined by an inquisition into our religious views and whether we are all coming back to the merry sport of frying astronomers. One might almost suppose, in reading the columns of 'The Times', that the works of John Stuart Mill and others had fallen into complete oblivion. The kindly observations of Mr Jenkyn-Thomas embolden me to make my own protest against the New Order now being proposed by many good Christian people, who imagine that the comely governance of our lives is impossible except under their special guidance. Their intentions are good. Some of their proposals are infamous.

For my part, harassed as I am with the daily problems of Evacuation (I mean Dispersal), I long to cry out with Confucius: 'Why do you ask me about Gods and Spirits? Pay respect to them, but keep them at a distance. When you have learnt to deal with your fellow man, then you may ask me again how to deal with Gods and Spirits.'[31]

The religious concerns, like the language concerns, were exaggerated out of all proportion. If anything, evacuees suffered from too much religious instruction rather than too little. They were frequently subjected to more than one form of Christianity, since their church attendance usually depended on where and with whom they were billeted. Although Catholic children were strictly supervised by local priests if available, religious affiliations were also dependent on the amenities offered by competing local churches. Opportunist evacuees were quick to experience temporary conversions when it suited them. For example, there were occasions where Protestant evacuees claimed to be Catholic in order to go on day trips, which were organised by the local Catholic church. Similarly, children would flock to the church hall which offered the best provision for leisure activities. Many ex-evacuees have also recalled that they belonged to the local Church of England choir in one area, but attended a Welsh Methodist church in a different area. Neither were children averse to using religion for their own ends. Mrs Winter was a young girl at a Catholic boarding school during the war and stated:

> 'It was the custom for the older girls to attend mass at six thirty each morning in the school chapel, and this requirement applied to me even though I was not a catholic. I really had little religious conviction of either a Protestant or a Catholic nature, but somewhere along the line I had picked up the notion that Roman Catholics were not allowed to attend services of another denomination. So I stormed into the bathroom one evening before bath time, where I knew sister was on duty, and burst out with an impassioned speech on how wrong it was that I was made to go to mass in the mornings. "How do you know" I demanded, "that we Protestants are not allowed to go to Catholic services, just as you are not permitted to go to Protestant ones and here you are forcing me to be to be disobedient." Of course it was a put-up job on my part, but with all the rules, regulations and regimentation of our daily lives I could not take it any longer. Sister withstood this outburst good-humouredly but nevertheless reported it to the headmistress, Sister Maura. The answer came back that, because of fire regulations, the staff could not assume the responsibility of leaving me alone in the dormitory in the mornings in view of the fact that the dormitory as on the top floor of the building and so, for safety's sake and everyone's peace of mind, I would have to go to mass. And so I did, with a little white veil attached to my head. That was a battle I did not win.'[32]

Precisely why *The Times* continued its obsession with religious education is not clear particularly since there were far more serious educational issues at stake. For example, most children who had remained in the evacuation areas were without education altogether. The President of the Board of Education Lord De La Warr, promised a concerned public that steps would be taken to resolve this problem.

> *We cannot afford as a nation to let three quarters of a million grow up as little barbarians, and the government have not the slightest intention of doing so. There are already some minor activities going on in the schools in the towns, admittedly inadequate on any long-term basis, but nevertheless something.*
>
> *We feel moreover, that the children in evacuation areas are getting the worst of both worlds. On the one hand they are running a quite unnecessary risk and on the other they are missing all social care and schooling, and a great number of them are acquiring habits of idleness, if not worse.*[33]

In April 1940, over 183,000 children were receiving no education at all and 13,000 were receiving less than half time instruction.[34] Board of Education officials debated whether or not to reopen schools in the evacuation areas. In the meantime, children wandered aimlessly in streets collecting shrapnel, looking for booby trap mines and swapping war stories. As crime rates soared, alarmist reports in the national press claimed that Britain was breeding a generation of 'Artful Dodgers'. Wartime air raid warden Barbara Nixon, in her entertaining autobiography *Raiders Overhead - A Diary of a London Blitz* (1980) tells of casual thievery by streetwise children, which she calls 'juvenile swiping.' Offered a box of a dozen light bulbs for the bargain price of two shillings, she asked if they had come from the bombed-out company along the street. She was earnestly assured that they had, indeed, come from there and that it was easy to sneak inside after the fire watcher had gone off to the pub. Gavin Mortimer, (*The Longest Night 10-11 May 1941, Voices from the London Blitz, 2005*) reports the Lambeth Juvenile Court proceedings against forty-two child looters. The youngest, aged just seven, had taken money from a gas pre-payment meter. Child looters were often the sons and daughters of adult looters and were sent into an area that an adult would find difficult to target.

The Times temporarily abandoned the religious bandwagon and caught up with more urgent issues. There were no new suggestions however, and according to *The Times* leader of November 18th, evacuation problems could only be resolved by making the process compulsory:

> *The core of the trouble was the number of people still in London who could not be described as necessary residents – necessary to its industry and to*

the care of those who had to stay. This led to congestion in shelters never planned as dormitories, and to the creation of undesirable conditions in many of them. More unnecessary residents have therefore to be sent away and comfortable and sanitary conditions created for the residue of necessary residents. The question is whether this can be done as long as evacuation remains voluntary and so long as no central authority exists both to devise and operate shelter policy. Much has been done, but 279,000 schoolchildren out of a total of 842,000 before the war are still in the evacuation areas, in addition to tens of thousands of persons who can also be spared and should be moved. By all means let the resources of persuasion – already extensively drawn upon – must be used to the full. The arguments against compulsion are many and strong. But in the last resort nothing can override the necessity for disencumbering a great city of those who involuntarily impede its war effort and for preventing vast numbers of children from running wild.[35]

The problem of juvenile crime was not, however, restricted to the evacuation areas. Police chiefs blamed the breakdown of the education system, a lack of parental supervision and the compulsory blackout for a serious rise in juvenile crime across the country. In Manchester and surrounding areas, local police forces imposed rigid curfews on children in order to combat the problem. Chief constables in provincial regions suggested that the school leaving age should be raised to sixteen years in order to fully occupy adolescent boys. Speaking in 1941, the Chief Constable for Manchester stated that the figures for juvenile crime showed an alarming increase:

The most significant fact is that since the operation of the Children and Young Persons Act, 1933, there has, with the exception of 1939, been a steady and systematic yearly rise in figures. During 1940 1,328 juveniles were prosecuted in connection with 1,241 indictable offences, compared with 746 juveniles for 735 indictable offences in 1939.[36]

While 'Artful Dodgers' allegedly ruled the evacuation zones, children living within neutral territory were confronting problems of a different nature. There was no official evacuation scheme in operation for these children and once the bombing raids began neutral cities were left in total chaos with no hope of respite. In Bristol at least 15 per cent of the population coped by temporarily evacuating themselves, others stayed put hoping for an official scheme to materialise. Working-class Bristolians tended to leave the city just for the night or the weekend and return to face the bombing when their money had run out, whereas the more wealthy members of Bristol society tended to evacuate themselves on a more permanent basis. The obvious class bias in this situation caused a lot of bitterness. There were also those who took advantage of the situation.

One clergyman estimated that 30 per cent of his parishioners trekked to the country each night. Some of these would go on lorries, where the average charge was one shilling a person, while others who could not afford the fare had to walk. It was estimated that several thousands of people left the city this way.[37]

Eventually, in 1941, some Bristol children were evacuated to Dorset, by which time they had already been subjected to nightly raids on a regular basis and had lost much of their schooling through sleep deprivation.

Even the BBC in Bristol was forced to abandon its broadcasting position in Whiteladies Road, Bristol. The BBC had already been bombed in London, and certain departments had moved to Evesham while others had relocated to Bristol. In the event of an all-out attack on Broadcasting House in London, contingency plans were drawn up to ensure that broadcasts continued. These plans involved the construction of an underground broadcasting fortress in a disused tunnel fifty feet under the Clifton rocks. Work on the fortress tunnel, which followed the path of the old Avonmouth to Bristol railway line, began in 1940 but was interrupted by the blitz. From then on, the tunnel was used by hundreds of civilians as a huge air raid shelter. Meanwhile, the BBC shifted its base to Bangor in North Wales.[38]

Amid this panic and chaos, there were contemporary observers who described the evacuation process as a momentous social experiment. Determined to capitalise on the situation, psychologists and sociologists initiated numerous 'scientifically' controlled investigations. This research was designed to assess the haphazard intermingling of people who barely spoke the same social language let alone shared the same habits. The investigations proved very little. An article in the *Journal of Social Welfare* confirmed:

> *The actual difference between the classes, as far as their psychological and intellectual make-up goes, are very small, even if the wealthier part of the population does not like to think so. The same is true for nations to judge. From the report which compares the French and English evacuation schemes, the French hosts and parents were faced with exactly the same problems as the English – return in big numbers after the first day of evacuation, problems of cleanliness, food, of worried parents etc. Here opens a very important task for the sociologist to collect objective data for the existing or not existing differences between nations and classes.*[39]

61

Despite the claims of psychologists and sociologists, there was another group who vehemently disagreed with their findings. Eugenicists were convinced that middle and upper-sections of the population were intellectually, physically, emotionally and psychologically superior to all members of the working-class. These arguments were similar in every respect to the Social Darwinism propounded by Hitler and his cronies. Notwithstanding this, there were politicians who avidly supported the eugenics movement, and their influence had an enormous impact on the lives of many children as evacuation policy took a new and unexpected twist.

Endnotes

1 Starns, P., *Nurses at War* (2000), p. 19

2 *Class in Britatin* (1998), p. 46

3 Ibid

4 US War Department, *Welcome to Britain,* (Sabrestorm Publishing, Sevenoaks) Originally issued as *Britain* by War Department, Washington DC, 1942

5 Quoted in Legg, P., *Crime in the Second World War: Spivs, Scoundrels, Rogues and Worse* (Sabrestorm Publishing, Sevenoaks, 2017)

6 Hansard, House of Commons Debates, 5th Series, 15 June 1940, col 411- 454

7 Flanagan, J., *Tears Twice Over: My Experience as an Evacuee in Cheshire and Somerset,* unpublished, undated

8 National Archive ED 136/125

9 National Archive ED/22/215 Memo to School Inspectors S. N. 645 16 February 1940

10 Interview with Raymond Banks, 2016

11 *Westward Ho*, Ministry of Information, 1941

12 *Living with Strangers,* Ministry of Information, 1941

13 Imperial War Museum ref 92/49/1 recollections of Mrs Betty Hillyer

14 Oral history interview Cambridge University evacuation project, EJ March 1999

15 Hickman, T., *What Did You Do In The War Auntie? The BBC At War 1939 – 1945* (London, 1995,) p. 138

16 Ibid., p. 139

17 *Dorset County Chronicle and Swanage Times*, 5 October 1939

18 Parsons, M., *Waiting to Go Home: Letters and Reminiscences from the Evacuations 1939 – 1945* (Peterborough 1999) p. 44

19 Interview with George Burt, 2017

20 Interview with John Hammond, 2016

21 Oral history interview Cambridge University evacuation project, AG May 1999

22 Interview with George Burt, 2017

23 'Film Shows for Evacuees' *Journal of Education* 2 February 1940, Vol LXXV No 1934 p. 96

24 Padley, R. & Cole, M., *Evacuation Survey: A Report to the Fabian Society,* (1940) pp.236-37

25 Oral history interview Cambridge University evacuation project, Arthur Jones 1999, held at the Centre for Evacuee Studies, Bulmershe Court Library, University of Reading

26 Interview with George Burt, 2017

27 Rayner, C., *How Did I Get Here From There?* (2003), p.54

28 'Leading Article' *The Times* 13 February 1941

29 'The New Crusade' *Journal of Education* 21 February 1941, Vol. LXXVII No. 1989 p 137

30 'Letters to the Editor' *Journal of Education*, 14 March 1941, Vol LXXVII No 1982 p. 209

31 Ibid.

32 Imperial War Museum ref 91/37/1 recollections of Mrs A Winter

33 'Re-opening of Schools' *Journal of Education*, 3 November 1939 Vol LXXIV No. 1921 p. 377

34 Hansard House of Commons Debates 5th Aeries, oral answers, col 885, 2 May 1940

35 *The Times* Leader 18 November 1940

36 'Juvenile Offenders in Manchester' *Educational Journal*, Vol LXXVII No 2008, 4 July, 1941, p. 2

37 Parsons, M. & Starns, P., Evacuation *The True Story* (Peterborough, 1999) p. 50

38 Hickman, T., *What Did You Do in the War Auntie? The BBC At War 1939 – 1945* (London 1995) P. 140

39 Wagner, G., *Evacuation' Journal of Social Welfare Vol IV* no 6 October 1940 p.107

Chapter 3
Overseas 1940

'I was told the Maoris would eat me!'
Tony Edwards, Sea-Vac, aged 7

Useless Mouths or Potential Saviours?

British eugenicists and some politicians had expressed an urgent need for the existence of an official overseas evacuation scheme long before the outbreak of war. At this stage however, the British government had declined offers of hospitality from the nation states of Australia, New Zealand, Canada, South Africa and America on the grounds that overseas evacuation would encourage panic and a spirit of defeatism within the British population. Nevertheless, those who could afford the fifteen-pound passage had embarked on journeys to the Dominions and the United States of America undeterred by the official view. Thousands of people abandoned Britain to seek refuge on foreign shores during the weeks preceding declaration of war and the exodus of the British 'well-to-do' continued apace once the conflict began.

By 1940, this elitist migration had prompted heavy criticism and considerable public disquiet. The plight of the British Expeditionary Force in Dunkirk had also highlighted the possibility of a British defeat at the hands of the Germans. Therefore, when the Dominions and the United States of America repeated their offers of hospitality, government reticence with regard to an official overseas evacuation scheme had partially subsided. An inter-departmental committee was formed, and the Under-Secretary of State for Dominion Affairs, Geoffrey Shakespeare, was asked 'to consider offers made from overseas to house and care for children, whether accompanied or unaccompanied from the European war zone, residing in Great Britain, including those orphaned by war, and to make recommendations on'.[1] These children were later referred to in the House of Commons in terms of 'useless mouths', potential saviours or ambassadors for Britain.

Right: Alan Corbishley was eight when he was evacuated from Southampton. This is the CORB packing list his parents were sent for his evacuation to Canada.

CANADA.

CHILDREN'S OVERSEAS RECEPTION BOARD,

45, Berkeley Street,
LONDON, W.1.

The following is a suggested outfit for each child undertaking the journey:-

BOYS.	GIRLS.
Gas Mask	Gas Mask.
1 overcoat and mackintosh if possible.	1 warm coat and mackintosh if possible.
1 suit.	1 cardigan or woollen jumper.
1 pullover.	1 hat or beret.
1 hat or school cap.	1 pair warm gloves.
2 shirts (coloured).	1 warm dress or skirt and jumper.
2 pairs stockings.	2 pairs stockings.
2 undervests	1 change of underclothing, including vests, knickers, etc.
2 pairs pants.	1 pair strong boots or shoes.
2 pairs pyjamas.	1 pair plimsolls.
1 pair boots or shoes.	2 cotton dresses or overalls with knickers.
1 pair plimsolls.	
6 handkerchiefs	2 pairs pyjamas.
1 comb.	1 towel.
1 toothbrush and paste.	6 handkerchiefs.
1 face flannel.	1 hairbrush and comb.
1 towel.	1 toothbrush and paste
x 1 suitcase - about 26" x 18".	1 face flannel or sponge.
Stationery and pencil	Sanitary towels.
Ration card.	1 linen bag.
Identity card.	x 1 suitcase - about 26" x 18".
Birth Certificate (if possible)	1 attache case or haversack.
Bible or New Testament.	Sewing outfit.
	Stationery and pencil.
	Ration card.
	Identity card.
	Birth Certificate (if possible).
	Bible or New Testament.

x No trunk will be permitted.

All clothing should be clearly marked in indelible ink with the child's name and the Children's Overseas Reception Board Registration number.

No Passport will be required.

Each child should carry a sufficient supply of food and thirst quenching fruit to last 24 hours. It is particularly requested that no bottles should be carried. The following are suitable and can easily be packed:-

Sandwiches, egg and cheese.
Packets of nuts and seedless raisins.
Dry biscuits and packets of cheese.
Barley sugar (not chocolate).
Apples, bananas, oranges.

From the outset, Shakespeare recommended an egalitarian scheme whereby school children between the ages of five and fifteen-years-old would be transported to the Dominions and America for the duration of the war. To this end, he suggested that at least ninety per cent of children should be selected from grant-aided schools since these accounted for ninety per cent of school attendance in the country as a whole. Preference would be afforded to those children living in vulnerable areas and those from less affluent families. The voyage was free for grant-aided school children and parents were asked to contribute six shillings a week for each child. By comparison, the parents of independent school children were required to pay fifty pounds for the voyage and one pound a week for each child. Trained escorts would be provided on a ratio of one escort to every group of fifteen children. It was estimated around seven thousand children would be evacuated overseas each month.

These recommendations received a mixed response in the House of Commons. MPs who supported the idea of overseas evacuation as part of a wider 'useless mouths' policy claimed that Shakespeare's scheme undermined this policy by the inclusion of older children. Simply put, boys as young as eleven-years-old were considered to be vitally important within the agricultural industry, where they were relied upon to assist with harvests. Besides which, they argued, British children were only required to attend school until they were fourteen-years-old before they become an integral part of the workforce. Clearly then, these older children did not fall into the category 'useless mouths'. Indeed, a policy of sending fifteen-year-olds overseas potentially deprived Britain of many able-bodied youngsters who could prove very useful to the war effort. The protagonists of the 'useless mouths' policy therefore, were disappointed that Shakespeare had not restricted his scheme to much younger children. They also felt that the scheme did not go far enough in terms of numbers of children to be evacuated.

In contrast, Labour MPs gave substantial support to the venture but voiced different concerns. They argued that, since the scheme included fifteen-year-old school children but excluded the same age group who were already part of the workforce, there was clearly an in-built class bias because only those families who were financially comfortable could afford to keep their children in education until the age of fifteen. Labour MPs did, however, acknowledge that this oversight was perhaps an aberration and was won over by the general egalitarian nature of the scheme. .

But whereas the principles of egalitarianism encouraged some MPs to endorse Shakespeare's scheme, they encouraged others to reject it. Eugenicist MPs maintained that, if Britain was going to send youngsters over to the

Dominions then these children needed to be the cream of British society rather than a random selection of all social classes. Their rationale was based on an assumption that overseas evacuation was primarily a way of ensuring racial preservation and eventual survival. After all, they argued, these children would be potential saviours should Britain succumb to a German invasion. As soon as they reached adulthood, they would be expected to join the armed forces of the Dominions and continue the battle with the enemy in order to reclaim Britain as their own. According to eugenicists, these potential saviours would need to be the fittest, healthiest and brightest of all Britain's youngsters. Following through on this assumption, they suggested to members of the House of Commons that, in order to preserve racial integrity, it was necessary to evacuate all elite groups and, in particular, British public schools. To his credit, Shakespeare condemned these suggestions outright in a speech to the Dominions Office Supply Committee, July 2 1940:

> I have seen it suggested in some quarters that it would be a good policy if some of our public schools, whose names are rich in tradition, tore up their roots here and settled down overseas. That has been urged even in respect of schools situated, as most of them are, in the less vulnerable areas of this country. The Government is fundamentally opposed to such a policy. Even if such a policy was desirable, which it is not, there can never be, in time of war, the available shipping capacity. Nothing would so undermine public morale as to grant such facilities to a privileged few. Such a policy would militate against the spirit of resolution and tenacity with which we intend to prosecute this war.[2]

Shakespeare also encouraged MPs to think of overseas evacuation in terms of the national economy and as a means of strengthening ties with the British Empire.

> There is one other justification for the scheme which is in no way associated with the war. It may perhaps be one of the blessings which will flow from the war. It is still true in our national economy that exports should balance imports. We are importing into this country the fighting men of the Dominions, and we are exporting back to the Dominions the best of our children, and for this double blessing the Mother country will be forever in the debt of the daughter Dominions. This plan for evacuating children overseas is really an invisible export, because who can tell what will be the far-reaching consequences of it and what the value of it will be? It may well be that it contains within its breast the germ of a wise emigration policy for the better distribution of the population within the

territories of the British Empire. That is what so many of us have been urging for so long and have prayed for. The dream is in sight of realisation. These children will form friendships, contacts and associations in the Dominions, and the silken cord which binds the Empire together will be strengthened beyond all power to sever.[3]

In his lengthy parliamentary speech, Shakespeare did pay lip service to the eugenicists, stressing the pioneering nature of the British race, but it was also clear that he did not in any way sympathise with their arguments. He maintained that his overriding concern was to ensure the safe passage of children overseas and to make adequate arrangements to guarantee their continued wellbeing within the receiving countries. These arrangements, he stated, were likely to vary between states. For instance, the governments of Australia, New Zealand and South Africa were keen to establish their own laws of guardianship to protect the young evacuees, while Canada and America were insisting that Britain should assume guardianship. Furthermore, although Shakespeare had stressed the importance of equal opportunity, when it came to the selection of evacuees, in the event this boiled down to equality of social class since the selection criteria were dictated by the receiving countries and not Shakespeare. Driven by their own cultural, political and economic agendas, much of these criteria discriminated against children on racial, religious and health grounds.

British eugenicists therefore, need not have concerned themselves at all with overseas evacuation because their views were already well established in, and enforced by, Dominion states.

South Africa excluded Jewish children altogether, while Australia declared that Jewish children from Britain should not make up more than ten per cent of the entire cohort of evacuees. The number of Catholic evacuees travelling to the Dominions was also restricted to twenty-five per cent and a colour bar was in operation in most instances. When the overseas scheme was finally given the go-ahead, systematic medical screening weeded out any child that was not from pure European descent. Children with medical defects however minor, and those with behavioural problems were also effectively excluded from the scheme.[4] At no time did these restrictions form the subject of political debate since they were never divulged. The numerous members of the very unwieldy Advisory Council of the Children's Overseas Reception Board (CORB) refused to get involved in any frank discussions about the process of evacuee selection. Politicians were not entirely oblivious to the situation however, as Mr Lunn MP for Rothwell was quick to note: 'In these cases of emigration to the Dominions, as we know, children have to pass through a very close sieve.'[5]

By comparison, the USA was less restrictive in selection procedures and even went so far as to offer mercy ships and change their immigration laws in order to allow more children to enter the country. The problem for both Britain and the USA lay in the fact that, the latter was officially neutral. Spurred on by racial preservation and potential saviour arguments Britain generally favoured evacuation to the Dominions rather than the USA. When the issue was discussed in parliament political opinion fell into two camps. In one camp there were the MPs who criticised Shakespeare for harking back to the good old days of the Empire and for refusing USA's offers of hospitality; in the other there were those who expressed considerable anti-American sentiments and argued that Britain was encouraging a refugee spirit by appealing to the USA for aid. Even amongst the military members opinion was divided. Rear Admiral Beamish for instance, was highly critical of the American way of life and the child rearing skills of American mothers. During a debate of the Dominions Office Supply Committee he stated that: 'there is a very good apple grown in this country known as the American mother. The reason it is called the American mother is that it only has one pip.' [6]   Beamish also claimed that American children were normally in charge of their parents rather than the other way around. Such insults were not helpful, as Major Braithwaite pointed out, 'I do not think that is the sort of thing that ought to be said in the Committee at this time. America has shown herself our friend and is willing to give us all the armaments she can, and to cast any aspersion in that direction is something I bitterly resent.[7]

Major Braithwaites' view was echoed by many in the House of Commons, particularly those who supported the 'useless mouths' policy. The fact that America was prepared, in essence, to take as many children as Britain could send, appealed to those who viewed the presence of children as a waste of good food in a time of rationing. Colonel Josiah Wedgewood, who was the leading protagonist of the 'useless mouths' policy was so insistent on soliciting American help in this matter that he sent his own envoy to America to offer support and guidance for evacuation schemes. The trip did have official CORB backing but the national press accused the envoy, Captain Cunningham Reid, of merely attempting to find suitable accommodation for his own family. This accusation was rigorously denied and there was no evidence to suggest that Captain Reid was in any way doing anything untoward. The war had generated an atmosphere of paranoia, both within political circles and the general public.

MPs who argued against sending children to America largely did so as a matter of national pride. They maintained that, Britain's troubles were her own to deal with and that Britain did not yet require a rescue mission. There was

FOR RETENTION

FORM AX(R).

CHILDREN'S OVERSEAS RECEPTION BOARD,
45, Berkeley Street,
London, W.1.

Dear Sir (or Madam),

CHILDREN'S OVERSEAS RECEPTION SCHEME.

I am directed by the Children's Overseas Reception Board to inform you that your preliminary application in connection with this Scheme has been considered by the Board and they have decided that.....................................

....
....

is
are suitable for being sent under the Scheme to and if the parents or other guardians of the child duly sign the form of application and acceptance of the terms set out in this letter, the Board, on behalf of His Majesty's Government in the United Kingdom, will endeavour to arrange for the child children to be sent to the country mentioned.

The general scope and character of the scheme have been explained in the press, by broadcasting, and in the information which has already been sent to you, but it must be clearly understood that no child can be received under the Scheme except upon the following terms and conditions:-

1. Consent to the removal of the child under the Scheme must be given by persons having authority to give it.

2. His Majesty's Government in the United Kingdom will do their best to arrange for the transport of the child to the country named above, for securing the care, maintenance and education of the child after reaching that country, and for the child's return to this country as soon as practicable after the war, but His Majesty's Government in the United Kingdom will not be responsible or liable for any injury including fatal injury or damage which may be suffered by the child or by any other person as the direct or indirect result of the child being taken from the United Kingdom, nor will any officer, servant, or other person as the direct or indirect result of the child being taken from the United Kingdom, nor will any officer, servant, or agent acting out the Scheme be of the Government who is engaged in carrying responsible or liable for any such injury or damage unless it is due to his personal wilful default or misconduct.

3. Though you may rest assured that every possible care will be taken for the safety of your child, the conditions under which the Scheme is operating are such that it is necessary to stipulate that no carrier providing the means of transport of any child under the Scheme will incur any legal liability in respect of any injury (including fatal injury) to, or any loss or damage sustained by, the child or by any other person during the carriage of the child from any cause whatsoever. By sending your child under the Scheme, you will be taken to have authorised His Majesty's Government in the United Kingdom to make arrangements on these terms and to have agreed that the child is carried by any carrier concerned on these terms.

4. The parents or other guardians of the child will pay to His Majesty's Government in the United Kingdom for each week following the embarkation of the child such weekly sum as the Board may decide to be the amount of the weekly charge which would have been payable if the child had been transferred from his or her home to another area in the United Kingdom under an evacuation plan, and the parents or other guardians of the

child/

-2-

child will furnish the Children's Overseas Reception board or any agents or officers acting for that Board with any information which they may require to enable them to decide the amount of such weekly charge.

5.   The amounts payable under the last paragraph will be paid at such times, to such persons, and in such manner as a Secretary of State may direct.

6.   If it is desired to complete your application on these terms and conditions, the application form attached must be signed by the person or persons having authority to send the child.   The Notes appended to the form are intended to give guidance as to who should sign it, but in cases not clearly provided for, or where there is any doubt about the authority of the person or persons signing the form, the full circumstances must be communicated in writing to the Board.

7.   It must be clearly understood that by sending the application form to the Board the persons signing it will be regarded as offering to send the child named in the form upon the terms and conditions set out above and will be representing that they have full authority to do so.

Yours faithfully,

ARTHUR MULLINS.

Both pages: This letter refers to the Government's disclaimer, which all parents wishing to send their children overseas via CORB had to sign.

also the problem of being indebted to Germany. Once the Mercy Ship Bill was passed by President Roosevelt in 1940, American officials approached Germany to ask for safe passage permits for children. The Germans scoffed at the whole idea of mercy ships being sent into mined waters to rescue British children, and expressed deep regret that America should see fit to abandon their neutrality. America had already declined to send food supplies to Europe. By saving British children while simultaneously allowing French and German children to potentially die of hunger they had pinned their flag to the British cause.

From a British standpoint, there was no real intention to ever take advantage of the mercy ship scheme. Officials did not believe for one moment that Germany would respect any safe passage agreement; though it had occurred to them that Germany might demand food supplies in exchange for safe passage. Either way, the prospect of having to deal with the enemy in this respect was repellent to all politicians. There were a few, however, who favoured the idea of British children being transported by American ships simply because this process might provoke an incident that would bring America into the war.[8] There were even more who believed that the plight of British children would 'tug at the heart strings' of American people and elicit sympathy for British war aims.

Whatever the merits and drawbacks of sending children to America and the Dominions, one thing was certain: the political climate favoured the acceptance of some form of overseas evacuation. The hasty British retreat from Dunkirk and the imminent threat of invasion combined to focus the debate. Thus, many politicians and civil servants had come to the conclusion that domestic evacuation was no longer adequate. The fall of France compounded the situation. As Shakespeare was delivering his report to the War Cabinet, news of the demise was relayed to Churchill. During the subsequent confusion, Shakespeare's policy was endorsed. It did not, however, have the support of the Prime Minister. The record of the meeting suggests that the events in France immediately took precedence over all considerations. As he proceeded to deal with the military significance of the French surrender, Churchill was oblivious to the fact that civil servants had approved overseas evacuations. He later voiced his unequivocal opposition, describing the plan as one which conjured an image of 'scuttling' under the threat of invasion. It was, he argued, both defeatist and with 'grave difficulties'.[9] By this time, the scheme was well under way.

Though unable to rescind the overseas policy, at this stage Churchill did make himself abundantly clear. In July 1940, a ten-year-old boy wrote to the Prime Minister begging not to send him to Canada. The boy was adamant that he would sooner stay in Britain amongst bombs than desert his country for a foreign land. The letter was published in *The Times*. Churchill announced that he was greatly encouraged and cheered by its contents.[10] He sent the boy a copy of his memoirs and wrote a personal letter to his father. Such views of courage and stoical determination, he argued, were an example for the nation. The boy was David Wedgewood Benn, younger brother to the post-war Labour MP Tony Benn.

Churchill was reacting in part to the huge popularity of the scheme. Whereas domestic evacuation had produced only a lukewarm response from the general public, the notion that children could be sent overseas was met with a flood of applicants. Over 211,000 applications had been received by CORB by 4 July 1940. Members of the War Cabinet became uneasy and insisted that CORB should emphasise the 'grave difficulties' of which Churchill had spoken. The scheme should be suspended, they argued, on the grounds that a mass migration would destroy the nation's morale. There was also a problem of providing adequate shipping and shipping escorts for the transportation of evacuees. The War Cabinet did succeed in temporarily suspending the scheme on 4 July, much to the annoyance of Labour MPs who suspected that the government scheme had been introduced merely as a camouflage for private evacuation.

But while the politicians deliberated, the preparations continued unabated, and on the 21st July the first evacuees to set sail under the CORB scheme did so aboard the *SS Anselm*, bound for Canada.

Ted and Eileen's Canadian adventure

The late Ted Stubbington was evacuated to Canada as part of the CORB scheme. His was a happy evacuation:

I distinctly remember that day in August 1940, when my elder sister, Eileen, and I arrived in Canada. Disembarking from the ship to loud cheers, we were greeted with flags, streamers, sweets and candy. It all seemed like magic! Here we were, a 6 and 9-year-old from London's East End, now in Halifax, Nova Scotia, complete with brown, fibre suitcases and musk name-labels. We had no idea why we were there or what lay ahead.

My story began when Eileen and I were collected, with no warning, from our home in East Ham, London. I knew a little about the war and air raids, but going away was a total surprise. I don't remember anything being said, but just, "You're going!"

Leaving our parents, we were accompanied by kind people from the CORB organisation i.e. the Children's Overseas Reception Board. CORB was a government initiative to safeguard children in areas of heavy bombing, by sending them to stay in Commonwealth countries overseas.

We travelled by train to Liverpool. After spending the night in a school (which had previously been bombed), we were taken aboard a 'freighter', the SS Hilary, to join an Atlantic Convoy of evacuees, for the ten-day voyage to Canada. The sea was rough and the journey long. Many children were seasick, including my poor sister. I don't remember much about how we spent those ten days, but I know that we were well looked after by volunteers on board. There were social workers, health workers, church people, as well as the ship's crew, who were very good to us. Our accommodation was good. I can still picture the white bunkbeds in our sleeping quarters.

We were kitted out with life jackets which we wore for most of the time. Being rather thick and large, they were most uncomfortable. There was only the one size, intended for adults!

We spent some time on deck doing Deck Drill. On one occasion, we had to remain on deck for the whole of the night, as something was 'happening'. I have since discovered our convoy was being attacked!

One day, a member of the crew surprised us by bringing a sack up onto the deck. He took from it a round shell, resembling a coconut. As we held it, he chiselled a hole in the top. Inside the shell were the seeds. This was my first sight of Brazil nuts. It was amazing! Today, that shell is still one of my treasures!

Approaching the coast off Newfoundland, there were many wonderful sights, including icebergs and whales. These are still vivid in my memory.

Once in Nova Scotia, we continued our journey by train to Vancouver, British Columbia. This took about five days and nights. I don't remember anyone looking after us or moving suitcases, other than the rail staff.

Many children were on that train and were being dropped off all across Canada. Occasionally, we would stop to get logs for fuel. The countryside went by unnoticed, but the prairies were something else.

I was really expecting to see 'cowboys and Indians' as I had seen some in films back at home. Completely mesmerised by these prairies, I could almost make out the curvature of the earth!

Arriving at Vancouver station, we were met and escorted to the ferry for a two-hour crossing to Nanaimo, on Vancouver Island. By this time, I had lost my suitcase. (But thankfully, it did turn up sometime later.)

At Nanaimo, a Mr. and Mrs. McGuffie greeted us. They were a kindly couple whom we were to call 'Uncle Mac' and 'Auntie Kate'. They took us to their home (appeared the best in the area), a farmhouse, which stood in acres of land. It was very close to the ocean so our playground for the next few years was the sea! (It's still there today; at the end of what has now been named 'McGuffie Road'.)

Once inside the house, I was immediately sat on the kitchen draining board, feet dangling in the sink and vigorously scrubbed! I was fascinated by the view through the window; we were surrounded by beautiful woods.

The house itself was wonderful. It had an oil-fired Aga-style cooking range, oil lamps as well as an oil-fuelled iron. There was also hot water. The fuel for these was Kerosene (paraffin), hand-pumped from a 45-gallon drum, which stood near the back door. It soon became my job to pump the oil.

Running water was obtained from a well, situated just above the house. This was fine for all uses, except washing whites. Unfortunately, there was iron present in the water and the laundry would come out a delightful shade of orange! On 'wash days', we would use buckets to get water from a spring about 200-300 yards away, up the road. The spring was about four inches deep. We had to ladle the water out, then strain it through net curtains to remove the 'mozzies'.

There was no electricity for miles, so we had no phones. We did have a generator in the basement for our electricity, but it was only used on high-days and holidays. We had a big 1930s cabinet radio, which was run by a car battery positioned in the back. It had to be taken into Nanaimo to be recharged.

There was no fridge. Uncle Mac would buy a huge block of ice (5' x 2') and chip off chunks to keep the food cool. We were very fortunate as our neighbours didn't have this facility.

Life on the farm was simple compared to our home in England. It was like going back 30-50 years. We were happy and kept busy with our daily chores and routines and soon felt part of the family. We loved having a dog. 'Tech' was a wire terrier. He stayed with us most of the time and was our constant companion. He slept in the kitchen. There was also a cat. Auntie Kate had a beautiful blue Persian.

Having already retired, Uncle Mac decided to go back to work when we children arrived. He had been an accountant at a wholesaler. Food there was bought by the crateful. We noticed numerous crates of food in the cellar. There were tins, flour and sugar, which had already been stored ready for our arrival.

The local community, being a farming community, were pretty self-sufficient. Being on a small scale, it was usual to have a pig and chickens, not herds of cows. Uncle Mac kept chickens, white leghorns. Baby chicks were bought when they were just 2-3 days old and were raised in a shed. After about 6 months, they would start laying eggs. The eggs would be transported to the basement to be graded, candled, and packed into trays of 24. Uncle Mac would then take them into Nanaimo to sell. It soon became our task to feed and water the chickens and to collect the eggs. It sounded like hard work, but we loved it! We never ate the chickens as Uncle Mac never killed anything.

After a while, Uncle Mac stopped raising chicks in the small shed. He then gave the shed to us to be our 'playhouse'. We had great fun making our own furniture from heavy, wooden orange and grapefruit boxes. These we cut and made into chairs and tables. We spent many happy hours in our playhouse. We played games, card games such as 'Snap', and board games, but mainly we played Monopoly.

We loved living by the sea. As it was one of our playgrounds, we had to learn to swim. Our first summer came, so it was swim-time. There was a large log across the cove. It must have come in at high-tide and stayed for a long time. The training gear for swimming was a length of rope and threaded through this were about six fishermen's floats, like doughnuts made of cork. Having the rope under my arms, I doggy-paddled out to sea. I found to my dismay, that all the floats had come off! I was very fortunate that Kate's sister, Ina and another person came to my rescue.

Once we could swim, Uncle Mac gave us his rowing boat. This was clinker-built. It was wide and very hard to turn over. The rule then was to keep 'in sight'. There was a gong made from about two feet of railway line hanging from a bent cedar tree. It was struck by Uncle Mac or Auntie Kate, with a steel bar. This could be heard from a long way off, so we then came running!

We spent many happy hours in the cove. I loved fishing. I have a photo of when I caught a big salmon! The bay was full of oysters and we often went looking for pearls. We did find some – they were shallow-water pearls. We saw many a Japanese family fishing over the cliffs and reefs. Complete families would fish for Rock Cod or Ling Cod.

People ate a lot of seafood in Nanaimo. There were bucketsful available. I never ate oysters, or crabs as Auntie Kate and Uncle Mac didn't eat fish. (I did enjoy eating salmon though, when my parents came out!)

Sometimes we walked around the cliffs to find that the army had been firing bullets. We kids found and collected the shells. We often gathered fire incendiaries, in silver and red, that were on the beach. We collected these in galvanised buckets. We also had fun chucking used army ammunition into deep water on the other side of the cove.

Unlike Uncle Mac, who came from Liverpool, Auntie Kate was a native of Canada. She had a cousin called Norman Godfrey. Going back a generation, Norman's family were among the early settlers in Canada. They were great landowners. I knew of a 'Godfrey Lake', a couple of hours' walk away. It was some lake as it was huge! The Godfreys owned this lake as well as all the land around it. It boasted its own cabins, fishing equipment and many other facilities.

The Godfreys lived in Vancouver, so they were referred to as 'townies'. They came over to Nanaimo to stay each summer. They enjoyed being with Uncle Mac and Auntie Kate, and they also loved the freedom of this local farming area. There were no defined boundaries around people's land. It was all open. One summer, unfortunately, I contracted mumps, so they were unable to come and stay. Norman never let me forget it even after several decades!

Eileen and I went to different schools. I started at North Ward. I soon changed to another school, Brecon School, after about 6 months, as North Ward was rather old-fashioned. Eileen being three years older than I was, went to John Shaw School, but we both went on the same and only school bus.

(Buses were few and far between. There was only one public bus. This ran about twice a week. It went from Departure Bay, which was an hour's walk away)

We both made good progress at school. I would probably have classed myself as fair, but later discovered from reports that we were both doing very well and were said to be 'intelligent' and 'well-behaved'. I always tried hard but I wasn't academic like Eileen. I enjoyed arts and crafts, and I particularly shone at woodwork, which I have continued enjoying throughout my life.

Uncle Mac hailed from Liverpool. He came out to Canada many years before we arrived. He was, therefore, not a native of Canada and I don't think he had any relatives there. He was an enterprising man in the community. He was one of the instigators to start a public library in Nanaimo. As an accountant, he fought tirelessly to acquire funding, quarters and staff for the library. He also audited the books free of charge. He was a leading man in the beginnings of the local orchestra. Mac played the cello. As children, we liked to make things. We had great fun trying to make a cello. We managed a three-string version using a cigar box for the sound box. I didn't get on with playing it very well!

In 1941, Eileen and I had our tonsils out, which seemed to be the thing then. Eileen went in to have hers done first, then it was my turn. We must have passed on our trolleys and I saw Eileen covered in blood. I yelled, "You have murdered my sister!"

Social workers visited the farm quite often, but I had no idea who they were! Letters then would be going backwards and forwards. They would always write a report on how we were, which was kept in a central file. Our parents were always informed and were very happy with all that they heard. The reports outlined our progress. This included our physical and emotional development, our health and our progress at school. Many examples of our performance were given to build a picture for our parents e.g. stage *performances at Christmas. Reports commented on the 'excellent home' and 'intelligent and loving care' we received from our foster parents. We were very fortunate in our placement with Auntie Kate and Uncle Mac.*

We loved the lifestyle, the country and the McGuffies so much that we persuaded our parents to sell up and migrate to Canada. On 7th December 1946, they set sail on the Queen Elizabeth, arriving in time for Christmas. Auntie Kate and Uncle Mac were pleased to support us financially until our parents' arrival, as we were no longer the responsibility of CORB.

Our parents lived with us in Nanaimo, at Auntie Kate and Uncle Mac's home for about a year. There were no docks there, so Dad worked in a saw mill for a while, but the working conditions were years behind those in England. He would have to work throughout a whole day without any breaks. There weren't even tea breaks. Even water was obtained from a bucket using a ladle!

They then bought their own property in Vancouver. Our attachment to Mac and Kate sadly became a bone of contention as Mum was jealous of Kate. So, the only way our parents could get their children back was by taking us back home, away from Canada.

However, Churchill's reference to the grave difficulties associated with children abroad was not pure rhetoric. At this stage in the war, Britain was losing an average of sixty ships a month. Indeed, the *Anselm* left Liverpool docks in a convoy that was attacked by German U-boats only six days later. The *Anselm* managed to escape but four other ships in the convoy perished. There were, of course, safety regulations in place for all children once they were aboard ship. No child was berthed below the waterline and organisers were instructed to make sure that there were no more than three children to every adult aboard. Children also took part in lifeboat drills before they set sail and again once they reached the open sea.

Government officials had duly informed all parents of overseas evacuees that both the journey and the subsequent settlement process would involve a great deal of risk. They also highlighted the fact that the sheer distance between these evacuees and their parents precluded any parental visits for the duration of the war.

In truth, MPs who were convinced that domestic evacuation had been ruined by over-anxious parents rescuing their children from reception areas even believed this lack of parental contact to be the finest point of the whole scheme! But, whatever MPs may or may not have thought about parental interference with domestic evacuation, they were certainly not prepared to accept responsibility for the safety of children travelling overseas. Given the inherent dangers, they insisted that parents sign a disclaimer form. This form relinquished the government from any accountability should anything untoward happen to the children. The need for this measure was grimly reinforced by an Admiralty declaration on 9 July, effectively alerting the War Cabinet to the incapacity of the Royal Navy to safeguard evacuee ships. Meanwhile, as parents signed their disclaimer forms they were blissfully unaware of the Admiralty declaration. They were equally unaware that some of the evacuee ships would become justifiable targets for German U-boats and the Luftwaffe since they had also been ordered to carry troops.

CORB officials had been forced to hire Dutch ships for the evacuation of children as the American initiative of Mercy Ships had fallen by the wayside. The Germans had informed the US that they did not intend to block evacuee ships, but the British were convinced that this assurance would soon be followed by German demands for American food and equipment. Certainly, an American ship was allocated to fetch 2,000 British children but a combination of bad

Above: The *SS Volendam*

SDL/18

CHILDREN'S OVERSEAS RECEPTION BOARD,
45, Berkeley Street,
W.1.

Telephone:
Mayfair 8400

CONFIDENTIAL.

Dear Sir (or Madam),

      I am writing this personal letter on the instructions of Mr. Geoffrey Shakespeare who is the Minister responsible for the administration of the Children's Overseas Reception Scheme. Mr. Shakespeare is sure that you will appreciate its reassuring nature.

      You may have heard over the wireless, or have read in the Press, that the Government cannot take responsibility for sending children overseas under the scheme without adequate naval protection.

      In the accompanying letter you are notified

      ~~You have already been notified~~

that your child (or children) has (or have) been accepted for evacuation overseas. You can rest assured that arrangements will be made for naval convoy. You can also rest assured that we shall not let your child (or children) go overseas if at the last moment we find that the situation has changed and that no convoy can be provided.

      In the interest of the safety of your child (or children), and others who will accompany them, we ask you to regard this information as confidential - that is to say, you should not discuss the matter even with your neighbours, and you should ask your child (or children) also not to talk about it. We know we can rely upon you in this matter.

               Yours faithfully,

Above: Letter of Reassurance sent to parents, assuring them of the
safety of children evacuated overseas via CORB.

weather and British suspicion prevented it from ever leaving port. Instead, CORB turned to Dutch shipping lines for help, though it was clear that individual companies were keen to profit from the dilemma. Shakespeare complained bitterly about the inflated prices being charged for the voyages: 'It does not seem quite right that the Dutch, whose future existence as an independent state depends on our war effort, should try to profiteer out of the British government for the evacuation of children.'[11] Apart from the profiteering, voyages were also extended by days and sometimes weeks as ships attempted to avoid minefields and evade enemy forces.

Despite these precautions, ships were still attacked. On 31 August, the Volendam was hit by two torpedoes, one of which did not explode. Children did not panic but followed their safety drill to the letter. One young boy of nine however, failed to leave the Volendam with his companions. His escorts overlooked him as he lay sleeping in his bunk and did not wake up until the early hours of the morning when he ventured out on deck. On finding himself alone

Above: Alan Corbishley was eight-years-old when he boarded the *SS Volendam*, bound for Canada.

he promptly returned to bed and slept until daybreak when he managed to attract the attention of a passing British warship. As one observer remarked, 'for a few hours this boy of nine was virtually in charge of his own ship, and no admiral was ever more proud of his command.'[12]

Alan Corbishley was eight-years-old when the application to evacuate overseas, to Canada, made by his parents on his behalf, was successful.

'I was evacuated on 26 August 1940. We left Southampton Central Railway Station at 09.16. Things were on the dot then, even if it was wartime! One thing I remember, Mum gave me something to eat, to take on the journey. She gave me a packet of Horlicks tablets. I ate them all before we left Southampton. So much for making it last! It was more traumatic for the

Left: The damage inflicted on the *SS Volendam* is clearly visible in this photograph.

Above: 4 September 1940, Southampton Central Railway Station. The Southampton area evacuees arriving home after the *Volendam* incident, with their parents.

parents than the children. There were two other girls and myself from this area. We thought we were going on a holiday.

'[The scheme was] instigated in June. The government sent out notices but we as kids didn't know about it. I think we had a week or two's notice [to get ready to go].

'Everyone had to know someone to go to in Canada. You couldn't just go over and hope to find somewhere. I did not know them. My parents lived in Maybush, Southampton. Just around the corner from us were another couple Mum and Dad's age who had a daughter, Eunice. He was a Hants and Dorset bus driver with a rural route, which included going through the New Forest. One of the stops was at Minstead Post Office. The post mistress had a sister who was living in Canada. She said to Mr Graham the bus driver, "has Eunice thought about being an evacuee?" He said, "I've asked her, but she said no." He said to my parents, "does Alan want to be evacuated to Canada?" That is how I got to go. I assume that my parents contacted them by letter in those days to say yay or nay - to Saskatchewan-Govan, Box 198. I never got there but we did correspond for 30-odd years, a Christmas card and a letter and a paper dollar each year.'

Alan joined the *Volendam* in Liverpool.

'We were billeted in five schools for a night or two. One school was bombed the night after we left.

'I don't remember going on board at night but I do remember the sea as far as I could see the next morning. I had only ever been on the Isle of Wight ferry before. When you are on the ferry when you are small it was huge! I remember having grapefruit for breakfast. We didn't have grapefruit often, so it stuck in my mind.

'I think we sailed in the night of 28 August, so we had a full day sailing and then half way through the following night, the 30 August, was when we were torpedoed.

'I remember sitting in the bottom of the lifeboat and feeling seasick, which is the norm. From the lifeboat onwards, I don't remember being rescued or arriving back. I vaguely remember being in a school when we were kitted out with clothing because we only had our pyjamas on.'[13]

Above: The SS Volendam on fire.
Below: Survivors arrive back in England.

85

U Boat Commanders report.

20.35   Convoy in view at 290° on westerly course, own course 90°. As preparation for underwater firing no longer possible, we circulated the convoy just out of view. When radio signal ready, radio signal received from U59 "enemy convoy at 5255AM steering westerly course". As it concerned the same convoy, no radio signal transmitted. At 2200 U60 positioned at port side of convoy. Until 2345, awaiting cover of dark, continued ahead of convoy and observed. Thereby established that a large ship, towering over all the other steamers, was moving forward in the front line. Moved in closer. Through closer maneuvering U60 now in central position in front of the convoy. Previously identified steamer sails in front row, second from left. Leading destroyer passes at distance of 500m. The target reveals itself as a large passenger liner with two funnels, 20,000 tonnes (Otranto class). Now to the right, position 30, next ship to the right, position 0. Owing to the very high level of marine phosphorescence, causing the boat to be brightly lit, it was, in my view, not possible to remain unseen and so I decided to make a direct approach at full speed, to prevent the target from taking evasive action. Apart from which, the distance between the steamers travelling ahead was at most 500m, so that I was forced to shoot at close range in the middle between both ships.

21.8.40
0000   56° 06' N
     10° 54' W   At a range of 250m, in position 60, fired 2 shots with a time interval of 6 seconds, while turning towards the ship, in order to hit the same hole (20 7C, depth 2m.) As a result of the marine phosphorescence the path of the torpedoes was clearly visable and after sighting the torpedo runs, steamer tries to take evasive action by turning. Therefore both torpedoes enter the same hole, level with the forward mast. At the first impact, large explosion and thick cloud of smoke, at the second impact after 6 seconds, weaker blast with a flame leaping upwards from the forecastle to a height of 10-20m. Then fire and forecastle is ripped apart. The steamer then sinks quickly, prow first. Diving alarm given, so unable to observe sinking. Shortly after impact, steamer is lit up as bright as day and searchlight from the leading destroyer, the steamer and a destroyer which has approached from the port side, reveal U60, which is passing behind the steamer.

0006   Emergency dive with ?. At 20m a destroyer goes over us and stops above us. For the next 3 hours, pursuit by 2 destroyers, 2 different locating devices heard, however U60 not detected. Occasional ? a long way off. Shortly after emergency dive several explosions heard, suggesting that torpedoes had been fired.

0307   Destroyer departs to follow convoy.

0334   Surfaced. Rain squalls, lack of visibility and heavy seas rule out pursuit of convoy. Headed south.

0400   56 8 N
     9 53 W   U59 log entry "Convoy scattered, lead ship steering 270 .

0625   U59 log entry "1 tanker of 12,000 tonnes and 2 freighters from the convoy sunk, in total 25,000 tonne Several more large ships retreated at 250 . It can therefore be assumed that some of the explosior heard by U60 after diving stem from U59 hits.

0717   Seas heavy, so dived for torpedo maintenance.

Above: The report of the attack on the *SS Volendam* by the U60's captain.

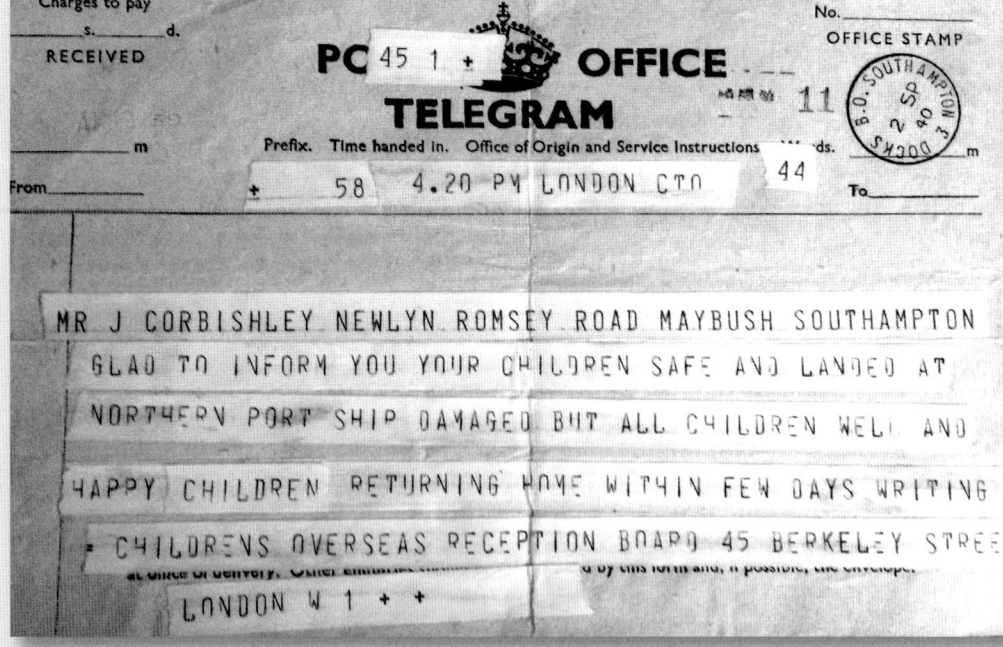

Above: The telegram received by Alan Corbishley's parents, telling them he was safe.

Above: The *SS Rangitata*, the ship that carried Tony and
Doreen Edwards to New Zealand.

Meanwhile, Tony Edwards, six years of age at the outbreak of war, remembers
embarking the *Rangitata* :

*'On the morning of 20 June an advert appeared in the paper asking for
parents to volunteer their children to be evacuated to the commonwealth.
My parents decided to put the names forward of my two sisters and myself,
and within three weeks we were told we had been accepted to travel to
New Zealand. I worried a little bit about this as my friend next door, who
was older than me, told me that Maoris would eat me, but it was going to
be a grand adventure!*

*'In August, the three of us left Bexleyheath station for the journey to
Liverpool where we were to embark on a ship called the Rangitata. I
carried my little fibre suitcase with all my worldly possessions in, some
lead soldiers, a clean pair of trousers, socks, shirt and a jumper. We had
to wait in Liverpool for five to seven nights before embarking and our
accommodation in Liverpool was pretty spartan, especially the straw
mattress, the hairy grey blanket for warmth and the bundle of old clothes
for a pillow.*

*'There were air raids every night and we had to stagger across the
playground to stand in the concrete above-ground shelter. It was chilly*

and bleak and sometimes we only just got back to bed when the sirens would go again.

'*Well, the great day arrived and we were to go on board the boat. My eldest sister was ill so she was sent home and so it was left to my older sister and me, along with 110 others to embark. On 29 August 1940 we set sail. I was in a cabin with three older boys and we left in the early hours of the morning to join a convoy of other ships.*

'*On the night of 30 August, the convoy was attached by German submarines and the convoy was scattered. A torpedo fired by U60 missed the Rangitata by a few feet and hit the Volendam, which was badly damaged but did not sink.*

'*When the alarm originally went, most of us believed that it was another lifeboat drill, of which we had had several in the two days we had been at sea.*

'*The attack took place in the early hours and we were woken by the sound of gunfire and the rattle of machine guns. Then stewards came and sent us to our muster stations wearing life jackets ready for any eventuality and from on deck we could see the torpedoed ship, now brilliantly lit up and with lifeboats being lowered down the side. For several nights I slept under the piano in the first-class lounge wearing my life jacket. We never did rejoin the convoy, but, in spite of all the worries, the captain did everything for our welfare. Even when it was touch and go, he saw to it that we were served with tea and biscuits!*[14]

Above: Tony Edwards and his sister Doreen were evacuated to New Zealand.

Most on board the *Volendam* had managed to escape without injury. Others were not so

Life on board could be strict. Tony Edwards remembers he received a shilling a week pocket money while on board the Rangitata but, 'we got fined a penny for standing on the rails or running on deck.'

lucky. The most serious disaster was that which befell the City of Benares on 17 September 1940. At 10:30 pm on that date the ship was torpedoed 6 miles from its point of embarkation in Liverpool, killing 256 of the 406 passengers and crew. Among the dead were 77 CORB children on their way to Canada, and six escorts. One survivor described the scene as 'pandemonium you didn't know who to help first, it was one the worst crimes of the war.' [15] Then aged fourteen and a private passenger, Lord Tony Quinton was also aboard the Benares, accompanied by his mother. He summarised his ordeal as follows:

'We were sitting in the lounge at about ten at night, thereabouts and I was reading an historical novel about Napoleon. There was a terrific banging noise which sounded, where we were, more like a collision than an explosion, but it was in fact the explosion of a torpedo somewhere near the stern of the ship. Then the bells went and so on and so forth and we nipped down to our cabin and got our life jackets and put them on together with a heavy overcoat and went back to our boat station. Then absolutely nothing happened. Then a rather energetic man said, 'I think we had better go to the boat.' So we all got up. Nobody came to call us. We headed off to where we knew our boat was going to be and indeed our boat was just waiting there for us, but it was a little on the full side. There were an enormous number of people in it. The crew began to lower it and then either a rope broke or somebody ran away from the winding thing, and it went. One end of it was held on by rope, the other end fell away and people fell down, and a lot of people just fell out and I fell out because there was an enormous weight of people falling on top of me, so I zoomed down quite a way. I must have hit my head in the course of it on some piece of tackle hanging off the side of the ship because I was not properly conscious for a while until I bobbed up.

'I fell into the sea. I came to, I suppose because of the effect of the sea, and looked around. All the lights were on the ship and it was a scene of vigorous activity and I really thought I was done for, you know, I thought 'Oh dear, well this is it!' and then, because I had forgotten I was wearing a really reliable life jacket, I bounced up and stayed up and then my mum saw me from 30 yards distance I suppose, and yelled in an imperious way and I swam over to her and clambered in the boat. The boat was thoroughly water logged but it was still buoyant because of the required buoyancy tanks and when we actually drifted away at that stage of the proceedings there were 23 people in the boat and I imagine there had been

about 65 when we hit the water, but the boat went, when it fell, bow into the water, not stern into the water, and was completely waterlogged so that only the bow and the stern were sticking out so that all of us in the middle were submerged. Well when the stern of the lifeboat hit the water it was completely submerged for a bit and we finished up with 23 people when there must have been 60 or more in it and of these 23, 1 think 8 were Lascar crew and 15 were Europeans. There were 5 children.[16]

Most of the *Benares* victims died before they could even move. Others died of exposure in the bitterly cold sea. Some of the survivors were not rescued until eight days after the event. CORB officials had assumed that, when travelling in convoys, surviving ships would automatically come to the aid of ships that were sinking. This was not the case. The Admiralty had issued clear instructions, which rested entirely on the degree of risk involved. Ships bringing up the rear of the convoy could only act as rescue vessels if there was an escort ship present or if there was no further risk of attack. The escort policy was such that, convoys were only escorted for a distance of 300 miles out of port. At a distance of 600 miles therefore, the Benares was completely unprotected, other ships in the convoy abandoned the area as quickly as possible. 'Certainly in the night one didn't notice the other ships disappearing, but they were right to do so.'[17]

Understandably, the Benares tragedy shocked the nations, the *Journal of Education* reported:

The doctrine of devils finds its fiendish devotees in Adolf Hitler and his crew. There is a pang in the heart of the nation. Deep sorrow, there is, and profound sympathy with the parents of massacred children as well as, for the moment, the hot rage and sickening indignation which is evoked by the latest atrocities of the gangsters. But not for long. The hot rage will be chilled into a colder sterner determination to put an end to this reign of terror – or to perish.

It would appear that relief was twenty-four hours away from the moment of disaster. It would be wise to remember in any tightening up of the Escort Scheme that there is now no depth of cruel savagery which the Nazi will not plumb: that there is no limit to his disregard of the rules of civilised warfare, and that future precautions must have full regard to those facts.

In this terrible incident, as in the incident of the Lancastria, (The *Lancastria* was sunk on 17 June 1940 off the French coast while evacuating British nationals and troops from France, soon after the Dunkirk evacuation.) *the quality of our children has proved to be that of refined gold. Brave discipline, unselfish consideration of others and unquestioning trust in their teacher and other protectors, have shone as a bright radiance in the darkness of a German savagery.*[18]

The fate of the *Benares* effectively signaled the end of the CORB scheme. Shakespeare announced the suspension of the scheme to the press on 3rd October 1940. Three months later in the House of Commons he stated: 'In present conditions it is obviously undesirable to resume evacuation of children overseas, but, as soon as circumstances permit, a further statement will be made.'[19] Attempts to revive the scheme continued until March 1941 but no one was prepared to risk another catastrophe. The government scheme was not resurrected. However, some children continued to be sent overseas by private arrangement.

The subsequent official enquiry into the *Benares* highlighted the lack of adequate naval protection and criticised the Lascar crew for incompetence. The Admiralty had forewarned the government with regard to protection. Furthermore, although some survivors had recalled the confusion that had been caused by language difficulties between passengers and crew, others spoke very highly of the care afforded to them by Lascars, many of whom had given up their water rations to ensure the survival of children.[20] Certainly, when survivors were picked up, the remaining Lascars required far more in the way of treatment for dehydration than did the passengers. They had also suffered the effects of exposure more acutely since they were used to travelling between England and Bombay and their clothes were unsuitable for the North Atlantic crossing. The official enquiry, therefore, did no more than vindicate Churchill's belief that overseas evacuation was far too dangerous to contemplate.

Before the government pulled the plug on CORB, a total of 2,863 British children had arrived in the Dominions under the official scheme. Canada received 1,532, Australia 577, South Africa 353 and New Zealand 202. No children were sent to the United States under the CORB scheme but 838 were sent under the auspices of the American Committee for the Evacuation of European Children with the collaboration of CORB.[21] These official figures are deceiving however, since they represent only a fraction of children who were actually evacuated overseas. In total somewhere between 13,000 and 20,000 British children were relocated overseas for the duration of the war, most as a result of privately-made arrangements. Around 84 'eugenically important' children were sent to Canada as a result of an agreement between the British and Canadian Eugenics Societies. In 1941, however, the Canadian governor banned the latter organisation because there were clear parallels between the policies advocated by eugenicists and Hitler's policy of social Darwinism, despite the fact that routine screening of evacuees entering Canada had been conducted along discriminatory lines.

Nevertheless, overseas evacuees were generally treated better than their domestic counterparts, primarily because there were stark differences in the way the CORB scheme organised, presented and implemented. In fact, the overall scheme was as much an exercise in international propaganda as it was of humanitarian rescue. CORB children were blatantly used to draw attention to Britain's lone stand as a fortress island against the enemy. It was crucial for British children therefore, to 'tug at the heartstrings' of other nations and epitomise the famous 'bulldog' spirit. Before they left for foreign shores, Shakespeare took the child aside and stressed the honour that was about to be bestowed upon their shoulders. Britain's expectations were voiced in no uncertain terms:

> If you behave well, people will say 'what splendid children these are! We must do everything we can to help their parents win the war.' When things go wrong, remember you are British and grin and bear it.[22]

Tony Edwards, one of these child ambassadors, remembers his arrival in the USA, en route to New Zealand:

> 'When we got to America, I remember being taken by some big American in a big car and being given fruit – bananas and oranges – which was taken away at the gangplank. They wanted to share it with everyone.'[23]

Great care was taken to present CORB children as part of Britain's investment in the future. While children had been previously screened for any physical, mental or emotional problems, their host families were also screened. In contrast to domestic evacuation, where hosts were reluctant to take on board children from the danger areas, hosts in the U.S and the Dominions clamoured and often competed to offer refuge to British children. Preference was usually given to hosts who were active in public life. In this way, CORB children naturally achieved a high media profile and drew attention to Britain's war aims. Moreover, the prominence given to the British cause effectively supplanted many of the social class attitudes that had dominated evacuation in Britain. Children arriving in the Dominions and the U.S. were viewed in terms of British citizenship rather than social class.

While internal evacuation was a domestic programme in which the lower-class identities of evacuees were highlighted, overseas evacuation was a programme of diplomatic international significance in which the national identity rather than the class origins of participants was emphasised. British officials viewed the overseas evacuees as 'ambassadors' of Britain who could help to increase international support for the war effort while to Dominion officials the children were not 'just evacuees, transferred from the range of menace but "part of Britain's immortality, part of the greatness of her past" and part of all the hope of her future.'[24]

Some evacuees were acutely aware of their ambassador role while others appeared to be oblivious to the burden and just settled into their new homes with ease. One recalled that:

I look on Princeton with delight. It had woods and streams where you could play, and right outside my house was a hill where I learnt to ride a bike. My best friend Skipper was across the road and I just became an American child. My sister had been skating at the local skating rink and she came back very excited and said, 'Mum I've found somebody to help with my maths homework.' Mum asked who it was. My sister replied that 'he was a very nice elderly gentleman who said he would help me.' Anyway she brought him back to tea and it turned out that this elderly gentleman was Einstein.'[25]

Undoubtedly, the educational, social and cultural opportunities afforded to overseas evacuees were by far superior to those offered to children in Britain. A recent study by Patricia Lin has also made it clear that, in most cases, good use was made of these opportunities. In some instances, the celebrity status given to CORB children ensured that they received more opportunities than their native counterparts.[26] From an educational standpoint, CORB children were almost certain to benefit from living in the Dominions since, with the exception of Australia, the school leaving age was higher. Moreover, attitudes towards education were significantly different to those in Britain. There was a broader curriculum and a more relaxed teacher pupil relationship. One evacuee from Lin's study explained that:

I believe that ordinary people in Canada were more interested in giving their children a good education than people in Britain. Most children even from poor families went on to graduate in Canada and all were allowed to go on until 18 years of age regardless of academic potential.

Another stated:

People's general attitudes towards education was that girls as well as boys had equal opportunities and that you were expected to be an achiever to the best of your ability.[27]

Meanwhile, Tony Edwards, having arrived on the *Rangitata* aged seven, found himself leaving school at a much earlier age than he had expected:

I left school and went to technical college. In New Zealand you start technical college at eleven.[28]

For some children, the positive benefits of a better education did not make up for the loss of parental care and attention. Homesickness was a real problem, and one that could not easily be overcome since parental contact was minimal. Their plight provoked genuine sympathy from Princess Elizabeth, who made her first royal broadcast to the evacuees on 13 October 1940:

Thousands of you in this country have had to leave your homes and be separated from your fathers and mothers. My sister, Margaret Rose, and I feel so much for you, as we know from experience what it means to be away from those we love most of all. To you, living in new surroundings, we send a message of true sympathy, and at the same time we would like to thank the kind people who have welcomed you to their homes in the country. All of us children who are still at home think continually of our friends and relatives who have gone overseas, who have travelled thousands of miles to find a wartime home and a kindly welcome in Canada, Australia, New Zealand and the United States of America.

My sister and I feel we know quite a lot about these countries. Our father and mother have so often talked to us of their visits to different parts of the world. So it is not difficult for us to picture the sort of life you are all leading and to think of all the new sights you must be seeing and the adventures you must be having. But I am sure that you too are often thinking of the old country. I know you won't forget us; it is just because we are not forgetting you that I want, on behalf of all the children at home, to send you our love and best wishes to you and to your kind hosts as well.

Before I finish I can truthfully say to you all that we children at home are full of cheerfulness and courage. We are trying to do all we can to help our gallant sailors, soldiers and airmen, and we are trying too, to bear our own share of the danger and sadness of war. We know, every one of us, that in the end all will be well; for God will care for us and give us victory and peace. And when peace comes, remember it will be for us, the children of today, to make the world of tomorrow a better and happier place.[29]

The BBC worked hard to keep children in touch with their parents across the miles and were particularly good at chasing up any instances where parents had not heard from their children at all, since letters were frequently delayed or lost in transit. Tony Edwards, in St Kilda, New Zealand, remembers hearing from his parents on the radio, 'I only remember hearing one radio message on short wave. I had to go to the butcher's shop [to hear it].'[30]

There was evidence too, that not all children lived up to the expectations of the receiving countries, even on arrival, as one official remarked: 'Occasionally, examiners found a cretinous child on board one of the evacuation ships, causing both Canadian and American doctors to question medical screening procedures used in England.'[31] The process of allocating evacuees to hosts was not foolproof either, particularly in the U.S. where some children were given to individuals with records of child abuse.

Furthermore, despite concerted attempts to allocate children to suitable hosts with similar backgrounds, there were the more familiar problems of class and personality clashes. Pre-emptive measures had been implemented aboard ship in order to iron out potential class differences but they still existed. CORB evacuees were given instruction in etiquette, taught basic information about the countries to which they were travelling; but such was the gap between British and Dominion and U.S. standards

Above: Tony and Doreen Edwards and their foster parents in New Zealand.

of living that a few children found it impossible to settle in their new homes. They were perhaps testimony to the fact that issues of social class had not been entirely eradicated by issues of national identity.

Nearly all CORB children were placed in families of higher social class than their own and it was only a minority who experienced class conflict. Indeed, at first glance, Britain's overseas evacuation scheme appears to have been more successful than its internal scheme but this was not necessarily the case. While it was true that there was not quite the same degree of conflict in the Dominions and the US, and greater stress was placed on a sense of 'Britishness' as children from the 'mother country' evacuees nonetheless experienced the same emotional traumas overseas as those who had remained on the home front. The scheme merely appeared to be more successful because 63 per cent of all

CORB children actually went to live with relatives or friends who were recommended by their parents. The relocation of the remainder echoed domestic evacuation in that thirty per cent were removed from their original host families and only seven per cent were successfully placed for the duration of the war. Even relatives sometimes did not live up to expectations. One child arrived in the US to be met by her aunt who turned out to be the mistress of a local house of prostitution![32] It was as well that relatives took most of the children since host families were not paid for their services until 1942. One woman recalled:

> My father fully expected to support us financially in Canada, but when the Battle of Britain was reaching its peak in September 1940, Churchill placed an embargo on all funds leaving the country and suddenly overnight we were totally devoid of our income.[33]

In reality, the overseas scheme was successful for one reason: it was far too difficult, expensive and time consuming for parents to travel abroad and retrieve their offspring. Most had sent their children abroad hoping to give them better educational opportunities and to this extent they had achieved their objectives. Politicians, meanwhile, had nurtured other objectives. At best, they had viewed CORB children as potential saviours and ambassadors for Britain, and at worst they had dismissed them out of hand as useless mouths. CORB children did not live up to these pre-conceived ideas. Luckily for Britain, they were not called upon to fulfil their potential saviour roles. None of the ex-CORB evacuees who were questioned in the Lin study, or those who were interviewed in a more recent study, had ever contemplated the fact that they might be required to fight to regain the fortress island of Britain. As potential saviours, therefore, they were nonentities. Indeed, at the end of the war a third of returning evacuees from Canada met with CORB representatives with a view to resettling in Canada, another third wished to do so if escorted by their relatives. Given the eagerness with which CORB children rushed to resettle abroad once the conflict was over, it seems highly unlikely that any of them would have taken up the British cause in the event of a German takeover. Lord Quinton was just one evacuee who believed that, had the Benares made it to Canada he would not have returned to his homeland.

> I should probably have gone into the insurance business, other people seem to go in of my type, in Canada and I would be a very vigorous member of Friendly Societies and Rotary and things of that sort. I think I would have turned in to an entirely different sort of person.[34]

For Tony Edwards, overseas evacuation permanently split his family. In October 1946, his parents joined him and his sister Doreen in New Zealand, having sold up and decided to make a new life for themselves. However, when they arrived at his foster family's home, Mr and Mrs Pryde in St. Kilda, with whom the seavacs had been very happy:

'There was a big argument. Not that I heard anything but something happened and the people who had looked after me never spoke to me again. I didn't understand why. The next thing I know, I had to go and stay in a room with my mum. My dad had joined the police in Wellington. Then Dad said they were going back to England. Doreen said she'd stay with the Prydes. About two months later, we were sailing on the Rangitata, the ship we had arrived on. We landed in August 1947, exactly seven years after setting sail. I was fourteen and going to England was an adventure.'[35]

It seems certain that for Tony, the notion of taking up arms for his country if necessary, had not entered his mind at this time.

As ambassadors for Britain, the role of CORB children was also limited. Members of the War Cabinet, along with CORB officials, had hoped that the arrival of British children in America in particular would sway public opinion enough to allow America to join the war on the side of the allies. The belief in Congress, however, was that Britain was determined to provoke an international incident in order to force America into the war. Furthermore, the fact that the British government had not deemed it necessary to obtain safe conduct passes for evacuees leaving for foreign shores in 1940 but later insisted on safe conduct passes for returning evacuees suggests that the Congress view was not entirely unfounded. A few politicians were willing to gamble children's lives on the possibility of getting the United States into the war.[36] In the face of this knowledge, congressmen were more likely to dig their heels in rather than alter attitudes towards the war in Europe. Therefore, although the presence of CORB children, both in the Dominions and America, was a constant reminder of Britain's dilemma, it is doubtful that this presence had any real impact on the foreign policies of the countries concerned. Neither was it accurate for politicians to describe these evacuees as useless mouths since had they remained at home, they would have become an integral part of the war effort.

The failure of political objectives did not prevent Shakespeare from stoutly defending the schemes against his critics. Speaking at Grosvenor House in 1942 he claimed that, over all, evacuation had provided children with a stable home, continuity of education and a healthy environment. 'The international children would be, if anything, ahead of the domestic because of the broadening experiences made possible by their travels.'[37] Recent research supports this statement. Interviews conducted with ex-CORB evacuees have revealed that at least 75 percent took advantage of their new opportunities. They subsequently climbed the social ladder in their adoptive countries with relative ease. In this sense, overseas evacuation was a 'profoundly positive and transformative experience, even for those who suffered emotionally and psychologically.'[38]

In many respects however, overseas evacuation was no more or less successful than domestic evacuation. The risks involved in sending British children overseas, whether as a political manoeuvre or as a humanitarian gesture were always going to outweigh any potential advantages to the children concerned. But those who were successfully evacuated overseas fared better in the long run because of the distinct educational advantages afford them by the receiving states in comparison to those who stayed in the struggling wartime British education system.

Endnotes

1 Report of the Inter-departmental Committee of the Reception of Children Overseas (cmd.6213) National Archive CAB 67/7/172, Minutes, 15 June 1940. Official CORB history DO131/43

2 Hansard Parliamentary Debates 5th Series, 2 July 1940, col 713

3 Hansard Parliamentary Debates 5th Series, 2 July 1940, col 714

4 National Archive, DO131/3 Meeting of the Children's Overseas Reception Board (CORB) Advisory Council, Minutes 16 July 1940, Official CORB history: National Archive DO131/43

5 National Archives DO35/713/M562-65

6 Hansard Parliamentary Debates 5th Series, 2 July 1940, col 754

7 Hansard Parliamentary Debates 5th Series, 2 July 1940, col 783

8 Jackson, C,. Who Will Take Our Children (1985), chapters 3-6

9 National Archive CAB 65/7/174, 21 June 1949 & CAB/65/8/179, 1 July 1940

10 The Times, 4 July 1940

11 Jackson, C,. Who Will Take Our Children (1985) p 83

12 Geoffrey Shakespeare speaking to the Foreign Office: quoted in Who Will Take Our Children (1985), p. 83

13 Interview with Alan Corbishley, 2016

14 Edwards, T., Unpublished account, undated

15 Mayhew, J., BBC Interview, July 1999

16 Lord Tony Quinton BBC Interview, July 1999

17 Lord Quinton BBC Interview, July 1999

18 Diabology, Journal of Education, 27 November 1940, vol LXXVI, no 1968, p. 211

19 Hansard Parliamentary Debates 5th Series 21 January 1941, col 70-71

20 Barker, R., *Children of the Benares: a war crime and its victims*

21 Hansard Parliamentary Debates 5th Series 25 February 1941, col 374

22 Fethney, M., *The Absurd and the Brave. CORB: The true account of the British government's evacuation of children overseas*, (1990) p. 89

23 Interview with Tony Edwards, 2016

24 National Archive DO/131/45

25 Raphael, A., BBC Interview, July 1999

26 Lin, P. National Identity and Social Mobility: Class, Empire and the British Government Overseas Evacuation of Children during Second World War. *Twentieth Century British History,* col 7, no 3,1996, p. 322. See also National Archive DO/13/45

27 Ibid

28 Interview with Tony Edwards, 2016

29 Princess Elizabeth BBC broadcast to the Empire, 13 October 1940

30 Interview with Tony Edwards, 2016

31 Jackson, C., op, cit. p. 87

32 Jackson, C., op,; cit. p. 90

33 Imperial War Museum ref: 91/37/1, memoir of Mrs A Winter (née Anne Westcott) who left for Canada age fourteen via Furness Withey Shipping Company 1940, accompanied by her mother and sister.

34 Lord Quinton BBC interview, July 1999

35 Interview with Tony Edwards, 2016

36 Jackson, C., op, cit. p. 196

37 Geoffrey Shakespeare speaking to the Pilgrims Club, Grosvenor House, 17 February 1942

38 Lin, P., op; cit. p. 333

Chapter 4
Suffer the Children

I felt a very sharp pain as the woman we were entrusted to grabbed the lobe of my right ear and then dragged me viciously up the driveway, saying harshly, "Right, I've got work for you."

Jack Flanagan, evacuated to Bruton, Somerset, aged nine

In the summer of 1999, BBC Radio 4 broadcast a series of programmes entitled *Evacuation: the true story.* Based primarily on research conducted at the University of Cambridge, the series revealed the extent to which many evacuees had been physically, mentally and sexually abused. Revelations which prompted a tidal wave of letters from evacuees who had suffered in this respect. The following extract is taken from a letter written in response to the programme, from a gentleman who is now living in Surrey.

> *At 9.30am yesterday I had to stop my car on the A3. I had just listened to your broadcast and simply could not stop the tears. Something I had kept hidden for so many years suddenly erupted through the pain of those stories and statistics. I was sent away at four years of age from my home in Islington. I was beaten, abused, intimidated and left night after night in a dark attic over a barn. I just wanted to say thank you for making this programme - it made me think, 'thank God that at long last its coming out.' I so needed to shed those cathartic tears.*[1]

Numerous letters expressing similar sentiments were received at Broadcasting House. Indeed, the response to the programme confirmed what the researchers had already suspected, namely that the numbers of abused evacuees had been seriously underestimated. Initial research based on the oral history testimonies of over five hundred ex-evacuees revealed that at least fifteen per cent of evacuees were subjected to sexual abuse and a further twenty per cent to physical and mental abuse.[2] According to these testimonies, host parents, priests, teachers and farmers made up the bulk of abusers. The question on the lips of those who were abused remains to this day: Why did the government let this happen? Why were they put at risk? Was this risk avoidable? Did guidelines for child welfare exist? Clearly the government believed that the prospect of aerial bombardment presented a greater threat to the child than potential suffering at the hands of host parents. This belief, however, does not excuse the negligence of placing children in temporary homes without making any checks on the suitability of host parents. Guidelines for child welfare had already been placed on government statute books in 1936. Yet when the evacuation policy was implemented in 1939 these same guidelines were ignored.

Video 31 Dee Williams:
A bully's comeuppance

According to the 'Child Life Protection' section of the British Public Health Acts, 1936, a person who cared for a child under the age of nine for reward was required to be registered with their local authorities. Officials working for these authorities were then responsible for approving foster homes. In compliance with the Act, they were also obliged to maintain regular contact with foster parents in order to monitor the progress and wellbeing of children placed in their care.[3] Civilian evacuation, however, had effectively undermined the notion of 'Child Life Protection'. Indeed, in the cases of children aged nine and under, the British government's evacuation policy constituted a flagrant breach of its own Act. Yet, despite this transgression, all independent child-care agencies were forced to operate in accordance to the 'Child Life Protection' recommendations. Ironically therefore, it was possible for a child to gain better protection if it was placed in a home by independent agencies than under the government's own evacuation scheme.

In May 1940, the Executive Committee of the Movement for the Care of Children from Germany issued comprehensive guidelines for the treatment, supervision and welfare of refugee children living in Britain. These guidelines stressed the importance of frequent regular visits to each and every child and their host parents, and the need for detailed welfare reports. These reports were to be submitted to the Executive Committee every six months. Moreover where possible, visits were to be undertaken by the same person who had been responsible for placing the child in its temporary home. With regard to children who were experiencing difficulties in adjusting to their new surroundings the guidelines asserted:

> *It cannot be too strongly emphasised that bed-wetting, petty pilfering, lying and similar signs of instability of character are sometimes symptoms of deep-seated nervous disturbance and should not be lightly dismissed or*

treated by penal methods. Most refugee children have undergone such physical and mental strain that it is scarcely surprising that they should feel bewildered and insecure in their changed environment and that they should find it difficult to settle down. Often their emotional disturbance is due to anxiety for the fate of their parents in Nazi Germany. These children become problem children who need and deserve kindness and patience to help them overcome their difficulties.[4]

Other recommendations related to social and religious issues and the Movement made it clear that: 'children must not be asked to attend religious services of any other denomination other than their own, nor should the religious status of a child be changed while it is under the guardianship of the Movement.' The Committee was also adamant about how to deal with child neglect or ill treatment, stating that: 'if a child is in surroundings detrimental to its general welfare it must be removed in consultation with the Regional Committee.'[5]

For the most part, it appears that refugee children residing in Britain were adequately protected. The Movement's published guidelines were usually followed to the letter. This was all a far cry from the scenario that had greeted the domestic evacuee. There were no specific guidelines in place to protect the physical, mental and spiritual well-being of thousands of British children. In fact, there appeared to be a naive and implicit belief on the part of government officials that all host parents would naturally be good citizens and rise to the challenge of nurturing the nation's children. The suitability of host parents to care for children was not even questioned let alone examined in any detail; and a lack of ongoing supervision left evacuees wide open to numerous forms of neglect and mistreatment. The ebb and flow of evacuation also created haphazard approaches to child welfare. Consequently, cases of abuse, mistreatment and neglect were frequently overlooked, both in the cities and in rural areas.

Child abuse was not a new phenomenon. Undoubtedly children were abused in a variety of ways before the war, but the unique circumstances of evacuation substantially increased the risk of abuse. By failing to screen host parents and provide adequate child protection, government officials had constructed an environment where child abuse could take place virtually unnoticed. This was not the only area of government neglect. Adult conscription into the armed forces had created manpower shortages and children were required to step into the brink. No longer viewed by the government as 'useless mouths' they began to undertake jobs that were hitherto performed by adults; as a result they were forced into highly unsuitable employment. Rather than protect children from this dangerous trend, government officials either ignored the problem or colluded with employers to increase the numbers of children involved. Once the value of child labour was recognized, the image of the evacuee underwent subtle changes. Instead of being seen as the scourge of the countryside, and the 'dirty vaccie' used by certain companies to advertise products, evacuees came to represent the young 'British Bulldog' spirit. People portrayed them as brave young children who had escaped the dangers of the city to enjoy a new, healthy and adventurous lifestyle in the country. Naturally this healthy lifestyle included essential farm work. Thus, evacuees were depicted as little heroes and heroines of the blitz romanticised in contemporary literature. But just as the 'dirty vaccie' was largely a myth, so too was the romantic vision of child labour in the countryside. Before looking at this child labour however, it is perhaps pertinent to look at other aspects of evacuee life.

In the early days of the war, the teachers who had accompanied evacuees into the areas offered most of them a degree of protection. The protection offered, though, was sometimes spasmodic and depended largely on the geographical area the teacher was to cover. Host families could predict with total accuracy when a teacher was due to visit homes and cases of child cruelty and neglect could be easily concealed. Once city teachers were recalled to the cities, or conscripted, even this inadequate protection was withdrawn. Not surprisingly, this process also undermined parental confidence in evacuation. Of those who had consented to the evacuation of their children, most had done so in the belief that the children's own familiar teachers would remain with their charges and keep a watchful eye on them. They were naturally concerned by the gradual recall of teachers and in some cases with good reason. Almost all evacuees could remember a distinct change in their treatment when their own teachers abandoned them.

> *We felt that our own teachers looked out for us, not just at the place where we were living but in school too. It seemed that all the trouble in the village was put down to one of us 'vaccies' as we were called. Once our teachers went there was no one to defend us and things got a lot worse.*[6]

The scapegoating of evacuees could also be detected in the log books of country teachers. The following extracts are from a Cambridgeshire school log book written by the head teacher. They express sentiments, which could be found up and down the country:

> *Dennis Manning, an evacuee and the biggest boy in the school, climbed*

over the fence into Mrs Green's garden to get a ball, in defiance of my rule against climbing. He was extremely impertinent to Mrs Green and I punished him before the whole school, two stripes.

Henry Coggin, an evacuee, received corporal punishment for cutting a table with a razor blade, and for cutting gates in the village. I doubt if this boy is normal.[7]

There was also evidence in school log books that Hitler and Mussolini did not have the monopoly when it came to fascism:

The habit of talking is still prevalent in the school and prevents serious work being done. I shall have to give corporal punishment for this intolerable nuisance in future.[8]

Contemporary definitions of child abuse differ dramatically to what was viewed as acceptable punishment during the war years. It was not unusual for example, for a child to be beaten by his father with a leather belt for a minor misdemeanour, and corporal punishment was sanctioned as a disciplinary measure within most schools, even though the practice was clearly a physical abuse of the child concerned. Significantly, school log books for the war period reveal that, compared to other pupils, evacuees were three times as likely to suffer this abuse.[9]

Claire Rayner recalled a particularly vicious headmaster named Mr Henderson:

My mother goes to see him when we are enrolled and tells him her 'I come from Kensington, don't you know' story, which completely beguiles him because, as we find out in time the whole town is enmeshed in snobbery. I also think she flirted with him, fluttering eyelashes and the like. Certainly he never attempted to hit any of us, though he was generous with his beatings for everyone else and always grinned delightedly while he was doing it, which I thought was horrible to see. He particularly liked an audience when he beat someone but after the first time when I saw him grinning while his victim screamed I never went near again when he did it.[10]

Mary-Rose Benton, in her biography, *Family Values* (1998), describes one of the sisters at the convent school she attended in Ramsgate, who evacuated with the school and found herself teaching both girls and boys:

We were to get to know Sister Vincent, at least the boys were. She never hit the girls, but she attacked the boys with anything she could lay her hands on. She even kept the rung of a chair for the purpose, a thick one, which must have inflicted untold damage on growing bones. Her favourite phrase was, "You little Heathen!"[11]

Some teachers chose to ostracise evacuees in other ways. One girl recalled the mental cruelty she suffered at the hands of her teacher who one morning chose to inform the whole class that the girl in question had begun menstruating and no one should sit by her because of the smell of blood. Not surprisingly, the child reacted with horror and embarrassment. 'I was mortified, and our relationship deteriorated into one of psychological warfare.' The persecution of this child by her teacher spilled over into her home life.

> *Miss W came to the house to complain about my behaviour at school. I wasn't cheeky or anything I just didn't say anything at school or participate much. I resented the fact that she was always so nasty and cruel. Anyway, Miss W sat next to Mrs B on the couch and said 'Lilian put down your pen', and I didn't. I was thinking I am out of school hours now and this is my time not hers. I was writing to my grandfather and grandmother to tell them how unhappy I was at school. The instruction was repeated but I did not put down my pen. Instead I ran upstairs very quickly to my bedroom but Miss W grabbed my arms very tightly until they hurt and I didn't understand why she did that. She said, 'your father was so brave, and he has lost his life for the war and he would be so ashamed to see you carrying on like this.' But in the end Mr B shouted up the stairs and said, 'for God's sake, will you leave the child alone? Have you not done enough damage already?'[12]*

Enid Philpott was evacuated to Bournemouth in September 1939, with her sister and found both her foster mother and her teacher a trial.

> *We were only there for six weeks. It wasn't very nice. [We went] to relatives of a neighbour, but she was well … I hated her. She didn't have any children of her own, and she'd say, 'I'm going to go out today, now if you come home and I'm not here you've got to go into the garage and wait for me.' The school wasn't very pleasant, and it was a case of if you asked, 'please Miss, can I go to the toilet? you were told 'no', so I'd go home with wet knickers and this woman would dry them in front of the fire and make me wear them the next day. I would have been eight then, I was nine in the November.[13]*

It was not just evacuees who suffered at the hands of teachers. One woman who spent her childhood in Birmingham during the war remembers her school days with horror.

> *They had just re-opened the school again after a long time. My house had been badly bombed and the bomb had dropped very near me and had left me deaf in both ears. When I got to school in the morning I could not hear*

a word the teacher was saying but she thought I was just being difficult. I was marched to the corner of the classroom and hit around the face several times. Every day for a week that same process happened and I did not even know what she was saying to me as she was hitting me. If I saw her now and I had a gun I would surely shoot her, she was so very cruel. In the end I just didn't bother going to school at all.[14]

Some children in this position were lucky enough to have relatives to whom they could turn to for help and advice. When evacuees experienced harsh and unjustified physical and psychological abuse from teachers there was no easy way of drawing attention to their predicament. Figures of authority were more likely to be believed and children's voices effectively silenced at every turn.

You just didn't have anyone to go to and confide in. After the war my mother was told that I had fought with my teacher and that I had been very badly behaved. I thought that was a wicked lie to tell my mother.[15]

Many evacuees who experienced abuse tried to escape their environments altogether. Some attempted suicide. A few would write pleading letters home to their parents. But unless children specifically mentioned in their communications that they were being badly treated, the abuse often went undetected. Furthermore, letters of complaint were unlikely to ever reach their destinations. Teachers censored nearly all letters and anything resembling misery was either put in the bin or edited out of the letter. This process was, in part at least, an attempt to prevent the tidal flow of evacuees who were flocking back to the cities on a daily basis. Some evacuees like Claire Rayner became accomplished runaways, she recalled that:

I developed a technique, I suppose you could call it, for not being noticed as a runaway. I would attach myself to a friendly looking person, usually a woman on her own but sometimes a couple, and say in a vague but unworried fashion that my mother and my sisters were further up the train and that I'd come down to this end to see if there were any seats. But of course there weren't. There never were. I would perch on the nearest piece of luggage and chatter to them in a cheerful sort of fashion until they were used to me being there. After a while I would say I was going back to the other end to see if my mother and sisters had found seats and set off to push my way through the unbelievably crowded corridors to the other end. I learned early on these journeys to listen out for the cry, 'Tickets, please! If you please. Tickets! Tickets, per-lease,' of the ticket inspector. At this stage the railways still tried to use them on their trains; later they gave up in despair, for completing the job of inspecting a train full of tickets in those conditions had to be hell on earth. But as soon as I heard the cry I would head for the lavatory. Even if there was someone in it, they were usually out by the time the inspector got to me; if they were tardy I'd bang on the door and plead urgency. It usually worked. The trick then was to leave the lavatory unlocked, and press myself against the wall behind the door, alongside the pan. The inspector would push it open as he went by to make sure he missed no passengers, but didn't push it all the way to the wall so he didn't find me. I wish I had the build to do that now.[16]

Like many evacuees, Claire ran away on several occasions and was re-evacuated. *The excitement of tricking my way back to London had been wonderful, but once I arrived I thought of my mother. I had to go home to her. There was nowhere else. I knew she would beat me. I knew after the first time she did it, that she would probably arrange to have me sent away again. But still I did it. Why? Because it was better than my evacuee life.*[17]

Jack Flanagan and his sister Mary were evacuated to Cheshire in September 1939. Jack and his brother Dennis were later evacuated to Somerset in spring 1942: *Our return to Liverpool was the prelude to a tragic part of our lives. In late 1940, the heavy air raids in Liverpool began. At the height of the raids my father, who was doing standby as a firewatcher, was killed just outside our front door. Two nights later, our home was destroyed in one of the city's heaviest raids. This was early in May 1941. The next twelve months for us were like living in the wilderness as we went rootless from one makeshift home to another. My mother, who was from a large family, had a sister living in Southampton who was aware of our plight. She threw us a lifeline by saying she had found us a house to rent in Southampton, but we had to move south as soon as possible as the property was in great demand, so we moved south with the basic bits and pieces of furniture that Hitler allowed us to keep. As the bombing raids in the south were still in progress, my mother decided to evacuate me once again. This time however, not with my sister, but with my younger brother Dennis, born in 1935. We were evacuated in the spring of 1942 to the little town of Bruton, Somerset. My Auntie Mary, who was a successful businesswoman, had the then rare luxury of a motor car. So, we all drove down to the completely unknown regions of Somerset. On arriving, we were greeted by a lovely middle-aged lady called Mrs King who was the evacuee support lady (Accommodation Solution Officer). We were immediately taken to the woman who was to be our carer for the next two and a half years. She lived in a modern*

Residents of this North London street desperately try to save what they can from their damaged homes after an air attack. Another incentive to evacuate their families if they haven't done so already.

council house on the edge of the town. The ladies were so impressed with this little white-haired woman with twinkling eyes who spoke in a broad Somerset accent. Tears flowed only too readily as my mother and my Auntie Mary climbed into the car for the journey back to Southampton. It must have been a stressful journey for my auntie as all the signposts had been removed by this time. As the car disappeared out of sight, I felt a very sharp pain as the woman we were entrusted to grabbed the lobe of my right ear and then dragged me viciously up the driveway, saying harshly, "Right, I've got work for you." She then took us into the living room where she laid the law down to us both. The fact that we had been smashed to hell in Liverpool and had lost our dear dad appeared to mean nothing to her. As we sat there in the darkening room, she laid down her instructions to us. One, we were not allowed at any time to use the bathroom. Two, we were not allowed to step into the front lounge. Three, we were not allowed to sit in the two spacious armchairs in the living room; her cat could but not us. I was only eleven and yet I was expected to chop up the wood, do the shopping, but worst of all, I was expected to polish the huge ugly brass candlesticks that dominated the living room on the shelf above the fireplace. To this day, I have a great dislike of anything brass.

Mrs Vines was in her middle sixties and had two sons who were both away in the forces. There appeared to be no Mr Vines and if there was, he was never mentioned. So, I had no ally there. In general, life for us was harsh and warmth and caring were very much in short supply.

I was expected to care for my six-year-old brother Dennis. Every evening I would take the sink bath down off the rusty nail from the outside wall, fill it with hot water and bathe him and dry him down. The little lad used to suffer from heat lumps, which would appear on the fleshy part of his body. I used to apply to these painful lumps something called calamine lotion. It would appear that they were caused by eating porridge oats and, in spite of being told, she insisted on feeding him on them. I never failed him, I never let him down. We were both expected to be in bed by 7pm, summer and winter. As we both lay in the bed and the bed heated up with our natural body heat, so the denizens of the bed would activate and soon columns of bugs and fleas would steadily crawl up our legs. The next morning, we would be covered with a rash of bites.

A rare luxury for me alone was for Mrs Vines at the supper table to present me with a huge chunk of cheese and a huge piece of rustic bread. I would sit there at one side of the table while she sat opposite. She would

*not turn the lights on and would glare in silence at me for the whole time
I was eating. As the natural light declined and the darkness enveloped the
room, her silhouette became merged with the gloom of the room and only
her piercing staring eyes were discernible. This was to be our life for the
next two and a half years.*[18]

Terence Randall was evacuated from Northam in Southampton to
Poole, Dorset at the age of eight. He and his three brothers found
themselves billeted with an extended family in Seldown Road.

*From the start it was made clear that we three were definitely
second or even third-class citizens. We sat at a small separate table
for all our meals and I remember that I could easily tell what we
were going to have for dinner the next day by looking at their
dinner of today and thereby knowing that we would get their left-
overs! I also remember that the food was not very wholesome and I
was often in trouble for not eating what I was given. Their
vegetables were always well overcooked and being warmed up
again everything was really not very appetizing and the breakfast
porridge was tasteless – this from a lad who had always enjoyed
his porridge in the past!*

Randall. T, WW2 - Recollections of My Life at this Time, unpublished

Around eighty per cent of the evacuees interviewed claimed that they had
written home to their parents constantly begging them to come and rescue
them from their misery. As one woman who was evacuated to the outskirts of
Northumberland recalled: 'I cried myself to sleep every night for weeks and
wrote to my mother all the time. After the war I found out that she had not
received any correspondence from me at all.'[19]

In fairness to teachers, it was difficult to distinguish between those children
who were suffering the transient misery of home-sickness, and those who were
unhappy because they were victims of abuse. In some cases, the practice of
censoring enabled teachers to spot child abuse. However, most of those who
were abused never wrote or spoke about their suffering. As one abused evacuee
explained, 'we children had no privacy and no means of real communication
with our parents.'[20] Another evacuee, who was not abused and was lucky
enough to spend the war in a camp school, pointed out that: 'obviously they
didn't want children writing home and upsetting parents. I don't think letters
were censored in a nasty sort of way, sometimes it was just part of an English

lesson. We were encouraged to write a composition or an explanation about something we had done at school.'[21]

Letters home therefore, documented the routine of school life, special outings, and films seen by the children or news about the latest fundraising events to be held in aid of the war effort. Grammar was corrected and evacuees were taught how to describe the countryside in a positive manner. Expressions of emotion, however, were not encouraged, and the nature of structured letters gave no opportunity for a distressed evacuee to ask for help.

Indeed, many evacuees have only spoken of their ordeals for the first time as a result of a recent research study. Some remain unable to talk frankly about the horrors of their evacuation. Others have found the process of recalling their childhood an excruciating experience. The following extracts are taken from their oral history testimonies.

My sister and I came home from school early one day because the boiler had broken down and there was no heating. It was December and we were very cold and hungry. There was a big container of apples in an outbuilding of the farm where we were staying and I took one for myself and one for my sister. When the farmer came home he took off his belt and whipped me for ages until I bled. He did the same thing every night for a week, then one night when he took off his belt my sister got a bread knife out of the kitchen drawer and stood on the stairs as he prepared to climb them. She was only ten-years-old but she stood and shouted at this huge farmer and he was really taken aback. He was pretty shocked I think. Anyway I don't know if our teachers alerted our parents or not but within a fortnight our father came and collected us and we spent the rest of the war back home in the East End of London. My mother said at least that way we would all go together rather than die with strangers.[22]

For some reason the woman my brother and I lived with used to talk to herself all the time. She was a bit strange in the head I think. When she was angry about something she would burn us with her cigarettes. When we complained about the pain or cried she'd say 'stop your moaning, the men fighting the war don't scream over a few burns'. I was only six at the time and my brother was eight.[23]

I was okay on school days because I was allowed out, but on weekends I got shut in the shed until bedtime. It turned out that the woman I was living with was entertaining another woman's husband and just didn't

*want me around. I only found out about it once I was moved to another
house in the village. The local gossip spread very quickly.[24]*

*Where we were, in deepest Somerset, I think the host family only wanted
us there for the money they were getting paid each week. In other words,
if they could save on food or anything like that, to cut down the cost, we
went without.[25]*

*The longest time I went without food was four days, but when I went to
school I kept falling asleep at my desk and the teacher came back to where
I was staying. There were a lot of raised voices but I was too weak and
tired to care about what was going on. I was moved to a lovely house after
that though. The lady there found me some toys and really fussed over me.
I stayed with her for the rest of the war and was pretty sad to leave.[26]*

*I was evacuated with my two sisters from Liverpool to North Wales. To
begin with I thought we were really lucky because we had managed to stay
together when a lot of families had been split up. But very soon the eldest
son of the house started to come into my bed at night and do sexual things.
I didn't know what was going on really, I was only twelve. He said that no
one would believe me if I said anything. He also told me that, if I didn't
keep quiet he said he would do the same things to my younger sisters. It
was not until many years after the war had ended that, I discovered he
had abused my sisters too and had told them exactly what he had told me.
I look back and think I wish people could have talked about that kind of
thing then like they do today. We were just so afraid of what would happen,
and so far away from our parents we didn't know what to do. It still
haunts me to this day.[27]*

*The farmer I was staying with used to come to my room at bedtime and do
all kinds of sexual things. I don't really want to go into detail but some of
it still gives me nightmares to this day. I did think about telling his wife who
was a lovely lady, but I soon thought better of it. I would have had nowhere
to go. Things could have been worse. A girl in my school got pregnant and
no one ever found out who the father was because she was too frightened
to tell. I look back and in a strange sort of way I think I was lucky because
I was only eleven years old and my periods hadn't started. I desperately
wanted to be with my mother but I didn't even see her for two years.[28]*

I remember during the hot summers, we did have them then, we would be so thirsty, we were not allowed any water so we'd drink from the outside loos. At one time I was so driven to despair that I attempted to cut my throat, I was ten years old – the knife was blunt.[29]

The neighbours had three sons. The eldest one was a few years older than us. He had some friends and the nightmare began. In the field adjoining the foster parents back garden he and his friends would gang up on us. First of all they made me lay down in the field on my back with my arms and legs spread out. They took it in turns to put twigs into my vagina, forcing my twin brother to stand and watch. Then I had to stand up and my twin made to bend over forward behind me and hold my hands with his hands and one of the boys would jump onto my brother's back and we had to let them trot around the field horse and cart style giving them a ride, then we had to reverse our positions. This went on until all the boys had had their ride.[30]

One woman who was evacuated at the age of three received appalling treatment. As a lonely, frightened little girl, Mrs Williams cried for her mother and wet her bed. As a punishment for this behaviour, the host mother brought the family dog up to the little girl's bedroom, put the dog collar around her neck, dragged the little girl outside into the backyard, and made her sleep in the dog kennel.[31]

I was left there all night screaming and crying. She done that every time I wet the bed. It became a regular thing. I hated it. I hated it when I went to bed and I would be saying in my prayers 'Oh God, don't let me wet the bed, don't let me wet the bed.'[32]

Another became the victim of a local priest:

The priest who came to visit us once a week sexually abused me. The family I stayed with would invite him in and say to me be kind to Father Michael. I think he was supposed to be teaching me scripture or something, I don't know. All I know is that, I could not tell anyone about what was happening because I knew he would call me a liar. He said that he was a man of God and I was a sinful child.[33]

Perpetrators of child abuse frequently escaped punishment. Of those who were brought to justice some received only minimal fines. For instance, a host parent who had severely scalded a young boy received a £65 fine. Another who had starved and beaten a four-year-old girl was fined £3, although there were others who were caught, convicted and imprisoned. By far the most notorious case of wartime child abuse was that which befell a small boy named Dennis O'Neill. Entrusted into the care of a Shropshire farmer, Dennis was beaten to death. His abuse was not detected because of the level of administrative confusion that existed between Public Assistance Committees, an Education Committee and two local authorities. The farmer was eventually tried and imprisoned for six years, and the government established a committee of enquiry under the chairmanship of Sir Walter Monkton to investigate the death of the young evacuee. A further committee of enquiry was established under the chairmanship of Miss Myra Curtis to investigate the ill-treatment of other children in England and Wales. A similar committee was established in Scotland under the chairmanship of Mr J Clyde.

The woman who was responsible for abusing the actor Sir Michael Caine was imprisoned. Under his real name of Maurice Micklewhite, Caine was evacuated from London to Berkshire at the age of six with his brother Stanley. Separated from his brother, Maurice was sent to live with a local policeman and his asthmatic wife. He was badly beaten by the wife and imprisoned in a cupboard every time she went out to the shops.

> *She didn't want to take me with her because I was covered in bruises and sores and she couldn't afford to let anyone see. A boy named Clarence was subjected to even worse treatment, and was beaten up by a tennis racquet and ended up with an arm and leg broken.[34]*

At one point, Caine was locked in a dark cupboard for three days and nights:

> *What saved my sanity in that dark cupboard was that I knew my mother would come to get me as soon as she could.[35]*

Fortunately for Michael Caine, a village school teacher noticed his bruises and alerted the National Society for the Prevention of Cruelty to Children. As soon as his mother received news of the abuse, she hurriedly travelled to Berkshire to rescue her son. Not only did she give the policeman's wife a piece of her mind, but she set about the woman with her fists and almost landed in jail herself! The host parent was imprisoned for cruelty to children.[36] For Caine, his experience in Berkshire left a lasting impression.

> *Fortunately I came away from there using my anger as a tool rather than a weapon. Although I didn't formulate it then I was determined never to put myself in a position where anybody could ever use me again like that. In everything I do, I always have to be in charge of my own fate.[37]*

To this day, the NSPCC remains Caine's favourite charity. Also, like many abused evacuees, the effects of his ill-treatment went beyond the mere stuff of nightmares. As his biographer, Freedland noted, 'He still shudders at the memory. He also hates being in a confined space. He was an easy-going child when he went into that cupboard. He came out tough and resentful.'[38]

Following his appalling experience in Berkshire, Caine and his brother were taken by his mother to Kings Lynn in Norfolk for the rest of the war. Not wanting to place either of them at risk again, his mother stayed with them to ensure their safety.

Mary-Rose Benton was seven when she was evacuated from Ramsgate to Stafford, where she was billeted with a family. Her foster mother, Jessie, often kept her home from school and made her clean the house. She describes just one incident in a catalogue of abuse while living there, after a visit from one of the nuns from her convent school, checking on why she had not been to school:

I was helping with the housework one day, when a nun from the school called to see why I hadn't been to school. She found me doing the dusting. Jessie gave a genteel little laugh. "She enjoys doing these little jobs," she twittered. [...] The nun gave her a sceptical look, told her, "You are to see that Mary Rose goes to school, punctually and every day," then took her leave.

Jessie was indignant that the nun had taken the care and education of a mere vackie so seriously, thwarting her in her use of me as a drudge. She would continue to make me skivvy at other times to make up for it. Meanwhile, she took reprisal, determined to enjoy giving me a sound thrashing. The details are very dim, but she was very violent, and kept hitting and hitting. I thought: When is she going to stop? She's got to stop soon. But she inflamed herself the harder she hit, quite uncontrolled in her language; the kind I had only ever heard in the school playground, but this time shocking to me by its association with violence and anger, and used by an adult. From being the mere rudery of little boys, the words took on a sinister meaning. My mother's swearing was only lavatorial or blasphemous, never sexual.

Fortunately, she grew tired of beating me, and poked me up the stairs with the clothes prop. "Yer've bin petted and pampered, you mardy bugger

People have asked me: "Didn't anyone see the bruises?"
Blows to the head don't show bruises. It's surprising how hard
a face can be slapped before the blood vessels break, and she was
careful not to stave me to any obvious point, but to make sure
I was distressed by it.
Mary Rose Benton, aged 7 when evacuated to Stafford

– go on, cry, I should!" And I was indeed, crying uncontrollable by now. I had never before met with such crudity from an adult, such mocking derision, as she jabbed and jabbed me with the prop. As I went higher up the stairs, I descended further into Hell.[39]

Peter Nobes was five years old when he was evacuated to Huddersfield with his three brothers and sister. Once there, they were split up.
I was given to a very nice couple but at first I didn't like it being taken away from my family. Once I became used to being on my own, I felt spoilt as I didn't have to share a bed and they bought me new clothes. I was well taken care of and enjoyed my evacuation but as I grew older, I always felt as though I wasn't wanted.

Evacuees were not the only children to be abused however, and it is important to recognise that some children were seriously abused within their own families by their own parents. Indeed, there were evacuees who actually managed to escape their own cruel parents to find peace and safety within the homes of their host families. The whole evacuation process produced a myriad of diverse and ever-changing social relationships and the role of the parent within these relationships was changing rapidly. In some cases, children were still protected from the adult world and the grim realities of war, in others they were expected to step into the role of adults and become an integral part of the war effort. Nowhere was this changing more obvious than in the field of child employment.

An increase in the demand for child labour in war time was not altogether surprising given the conscription of the adult population into the armed forces. The Defence Regulations of 1939 allowed for the employment of children from thirteen years upwards, but industry began agitating for a change in the laws that governed child labour from the outset. In July 1940, for instance, representatives of the Staffordshire pottery workers approached local education authorities to ask if young children could be released from school to work in the potteries. The request was denied. However, local education authorities appeared to be more sympathetic to requests from farmers for help with the harvest. Indeed, the Board of Education was forced to intervene on several occasions when some authorities proposed to allow school children younger than thirteen years of age to be released for farm work. This intervention, though highly appropriate, proved to be extremely unpopular, not only with the farming community but also with the general public. Even in religious quarters, where some support for the notion of child protection might be expected, the Board of Education was criticised. The Bishop of Gloucester wrote a strongly worded letter to *The Times* proclaiming that the Board of Education was totally in the wrong to block the release of young school children for land work.

The *Journal of Education* was quick to point out that:

The Board of Education is bound by the law quite as tightly as is the man in the street or even the Bishop of Gloucester himself. If the Board of Education had, without change of legislation, concurred in these proposed breaches of the law, they would indeed have been held to be blameworthy and their action would undoubtedly have been challenged.[40]

There were, of course, good reasons why the Board of Education needed to step in and protect children from being used and abused in the work environment, particularly in agriculture where protective legislation was non-existent. As a young boy, Michael Caine narrowly escaped injury from farm animals on several occasions and remembered a young farmer's boy who was trampled to death by a horse. Caine himself used to help with the sheep shearing and was shot in the leg by a twelve-bore shot gun while on a pheasant beat.[41]

The countryside can be a violent place. You'd never suspect just how vicious cows get when they go mad. I'll never forget seeing one go straight through a barbed wire fence like a runaway tank.[42]

It was not only the animals that made agricultural work a risky enterprise for children. On 20 September 1940, an inquest was held at Addenbrookes Hospital into the death of a ten-year-old Cambridgeshire boy named Anthony Thomas Burling. A theory was put forward that the boy had injured himself whilst chasing a rabbit. He had supposedly fallen on a tree stump and sustained fatal crush injuries. His father, who claimed that at 6pm on 11 September his son had been ploughing using a tractor on his land, identified his body. 'Although only ten he was accustomed to ploughing and was very capable with the tractor.'[43]

This particular case was typical of numerous others across the country. In fact, the lack of protection for children working in agriculture at this time amounted to a national scandal. But while the number of farm accidents involving children increased sharply throughout the war statistics are not reliable. Even before the war information about children working in agriculture was difficult to obtain. The International Labour Office had noted in its Geneva Conference of February 1938:

The British government would appear to have left a considerable gap in the system of child protection by the exclusion of agriculture from all legislation in this respect, while farmers, in view of the considerable importance of child labour during certain periods of agricultural production and in certain forms of agricultural undertakings, have opposed such legislation... During its systematic research for further information on which to draft the present report the Office had to realise that such information bearing on the amount of child labour in agriculture and its probable evolution are very scattered and often missing or not up to date.[44]

The Report of the International Labour Office concluded that, 'children are employed in a wide extent in agriculture and in certain collective and individual operations which are harming them physically and which limit their intellectual development.'[45] They also pointed out that since legislation was non-existent in most countries, the only way to prevent children being exploited on the land was to enforce school attendance laws.[46]

In Britain, terms and conditions for the employment of children in agriculture were laid in the Defence (Agriculture and Fisheries) Regulations of 1939. Regulation 29 and 30 of the Defence Regulations allowed for the employment of children aged thirteen years and over in agriculture under safeguards. But, in 1942, an Order in Council added to these Regulations giving local education authorities the right to exempt children aged twelve years and over from school attendance, should they be needed to work on local farms. The exemption was limited to twenty half days a year. In the event, there were very few farmers who abided by this ruling and children as young as five were to be found working the land. By 1942, the percentage of school absenteeism had doubled from its pre-war figure.[47]

With the introduction of the new Order in Council, battle lines were effectively drawn between educationalists and farmers. Sir Percival Sharp expressed his concerns as follows:

It is unfortunate that the granting of this power to a servant of the Board of Education is not explicitly given. It is implicit and even only remotely implicit. The conditions or circumstances under which His Majesty's Inspector may extend this period of exemption are not specified in the Order. Nor is the period of the extension of the exemption either specified or limited. In effect, this gives to an officer of the Board of Education, by a singularly unsatisfactory drafting of the Order of Council, a power which goes far beyond that of the local education authority.

It is to be hoped that the local education authorities, before becoming parties to any break in the child's schooling will thoroughly satisfy themselves that the interest of the country would suffer by refusing to sanction such a break.

> *These children who are to be permitted to work on the land at the age of twelve will mainly be found in reception areas, and a substantial proportion of these will be children who have been evacuated to those areas. The Order provides that the consent of the father or mother of the child or the person having actual custody shall be necessary before entry into child labour. On the wording of the order it would appear that an evacuated child may be thrown into child labour by a person other than his parent. These parents have fallen in with the policy of evacuating their children but they should not be put in the position of being powerless to prevent their children from entering into child labour at the instances of a third party.*[48]

These concerns were well founded since many parents had absolutely no say in whether or not their children worked on the land. A spokesman for Middlesex Education Committee supported Sir Percival's view and pointed out that:

> *For the past fifty years we have been building up walls of safeguard between the child and certain classes of grasping industrialists. Children of ten and over no longer have to work in factories from six until twelve and go to school in the afternoon, and the age at which they can go to work has been gradually raised. Hitler has conscripted all the young children from the age of ten: we do not have conscription, but this regulation is the first breach in the safeguards.*[49]

Despite the concerns of educationalists, there was a good deal of sympathy and support for farmers. It can be argued, though, that much of this sympathy was based on genuine fears of potential food shortages should crops be left unharvested. Nevertheless, there were other reasons why the general public seemed to support the employment of children in agriculture. For one thing, it appeared to be a healthy occupation. Children working in the open air did not conjure up the same image as children working in grimy factories and mines. Therefore, while the general public were likely to openly condemn the use of young children in certain industrial occupations, they were far less likely to object to their working on the land. Despite the fact that farm machinery could be just as dangerous to operate as factory machinery, the image of children harvesting the crops was imbued with a patriotic sentimentality. This attitude was not unique to Britain. As sociologist Viviana Zelizer has stated:

> *Although Americans began to condemn industrial child labour, most still believed farming 'almost blindly and romantically' to be 'good work'*

'Good' farm work took place on family farms with parents as part of the child's agricultural education. Thus, children's war work on the farm front during World War Two continued to be considered 'good work' but now necessary for the 'good war.'[50]

Echoing these views, a large proportion of the British public believed that children could and should pull their weight, however slight, on the nation's farms. They equally believed that children would be fitter and healthier for doing so. Stating the case for farmers, Mr Eddie Williams from Blackwood wrote to the editor of the *Journal of Education*:

Dear Sir,

Sir Percival Sharp in his article 'Children on the Land' rightly proclaims that the child of twelve today is a defenceless creature and calls for care. I quite agree, and since this war began I have been far more worried over his body than his mind, and still regard body neglect a far greater danger than brain development neglect. It is such nonsense to keep reiterating that education is the first casualty. It is a lack of food that could bring the whole structure toppling down and defeating us. On this summer's harvest and next autumn's crops and next winter's milk and vegetables the future of our country is going to depend. We cannot afford to take chances. Results will be proportionate to the use of all our resources human as well as chemical and mechanical. No workers, tractors, implements, fertilisers should stand idle nor, in my opinion, strong healthy enthusiastic boys and girls who are burning to help and have obtained permission from their parents or guardians.

There will be no education for any of these boys or girls if Hitler and his horde defeat us and therefore it is nonsensical to forbid these boys and girls to pull their weight in our common cause against a ruthless and merciless foe when they show they are so eager.

It is only fair for us to look at the question through the eyes of the fathers in the forces. When the German soldiers went home on leave during the Great War and found their families more or less starving they decided it was foolish to fight on and be party to the slow death of their children. We don't want that to happen here, and so we must use all our powers to prevent it.

Therefore I support the joint agreement of the Ministry of Agriculture and the Board of Education to regularise the employment of boys and girls ages 12 to 14 subject to a maximum of 29 school sessions per annum, and to the parents' consent being given, and to the boys and girls being suitably shod and clad, and to due recompense being paid. I think we can safely leave it to their teachers to see they are not exploited. We need not be over suspicious.[50]

Of course, it was totally naive to believe that teachers could prevent their pupils from being exploited. For the most part, teachers had little or no say in school attendance whatsoever, merely recording in school log books that attendance was low due to the potato picking season or other crops being harvested, although some dutiful teachers joined their senior pupils working the land in order to keep a close eye on what was being asked of them. The following is a report from an evacuated teacher working in the merged Littleport and Bethnal Green Boys School:

The Senior Boys of Littleport School including myself have been liberated from school to work on the land during most of autumn. Some have been driving beet-carts and some have been with a potato gang. Those with the potato gang are picking, cob catching or leading away. Those picking, gather the potatoes and put them into cobs which are large baskets. All the pickers have a retch which is their part of the field to pick. The spinner goes in front and spins out the potatoes, and as the spinner goes past their retch they start picking, when they have picked one side of their retch the cart comes along and picks up the potatoes. Many of the senior boys were helping in the wheat harvest earlier in the year. Besides cob-catching there are boys who have been beet carting and helping to get up the celery.[51]

Significantly, school log books from 1940 until the end of the war indicate that there was no time limit on the number of hours worked by pupils. The above report was written before amendment to the Defence Regulations, which, in theory, restricted the hours of child labour to the equivalent of twenty half days a year. These restrictions were flouted at every turn.

Given the circumstances of war it was not unreasonable to expect children to work the land if they were fit and healthy, over twelve years of age, appropriately attired and instructed and carefully supervised. Indeed, many enjoyed the experience. But it was a different matter entirely to expect small children aged between five and twelve years to assist in harvesting crops and operating farm machinery. Herein lay the problem. Small children were often used and abused because, even in areas where protective legislation existed, such legislation was not enforced.

Not for the first time central government had abdicated its responsibility towards children and offloaded the problem onto local education authorities.

Though in fairness to central government, it was reasonable to an extent, to expect each authority to adjust its child employment policies to local conditions. Within the remit of the central laws governing child labour, each authority was expected to respond to farmer's demands as they saw fit, but very few provided or enforced any legislation to control the employment of children in agriculture. They merely released children from school according to the seasonal demands from farmers. There were frequently no safeguards and no supervision of the work involved. Some authorities, like Kettering, took a hard line in support of education and resolved 'not to exercise the power conferred on them under the Defence Regulation to exempt children of school age from school attendance to engage in agricultural work of a seasonal nature, and that schools be closed for the ordinary summer holiday period during the month of August.'[53]

Others, such as Leicestershire, laid down rigid guidelines. School children in Leicestershire were only allowed to work with parental consent, and between the hours of 8.45 am and 4.30 pm. They were not allowed to work in adverse weather conditions and elementary school children were not allowed to work more than three days in any week. In addition, minimum hourly rates were agreed of 8d for boys over the age of sixteen and 6d under sixteen, and 7d for girls under the age of sixteen and 5½d under sixteen. Farmers paid an extra penny an hour for each child to the War Agriculture Executive Committee for insurance purposes. No requests were to be accepted if they were made direct to individual schools. The Education Committee in Leicestershire was adamant that: 'there will be control over the employment and no exploitation.'[52]

Meanwhile, official government radio broadcasts continually stressed the need for child labour and promoted a 'Lend a Hand on the Land' campaign. With Ministry of Information propaganda saying one thing and the Board of Education another, parents were understandably confused. On 19 May 1942 Gainsborough police court reported that a number of parents were facing prosecution for keeping their children away from school but many had considered they were free to do this.[53] Moreover, a protracted rise in absenteeism suggested that officials at the Board of Education were fighting a losing battle. They warned several authorities, such as Herefordshire and Shropshire, that funding would be withheld if they continued to flout the child school exemption rules, but authorities frequently ignored these warnings. The President of the Board attempted to appease worried teachers and child protection agencies by equating children's war work with notions of citizenship and religious education. Speaking to teachers and representatives of local education authorities in Lincoln he claimed:

The schools and scholars have been brought more into the life of the nation through the share which they have taken and are taking in our war effort. Children are doing their bit by helping with salvage work, the collection of waste, school savings groups, digging for victory, making comforts for troops and adopting ships. All this practical work and practical service is worth many a class-room lesson in citizenship. They offer the first beginning of teaching children to realise they have something to give to the common stock. Indeed, I believe that activities of this kind may well be ancillary to the religious education which we are anxious should have its rightful place in the life of schools, inasmuch as Christianity is not only a faith to be followed but a life to be lived.[54]

In truth, Board of Education officials had realised that they had very little political clout compared with members of other government departments with ministerial responsibilities. Consequently, not only were they unable to protect children from unsuitable labour in agriculture they even went so far as to sanction unsuitable labour at school. In a circular entitled 'Some Autumn Tasks for School Children' the Board requested the assistance of school children in collecting a plant named Colchicum Autumnale L for the Ministry of Health. The herb, which was also known as meadow saffron or autumn crocus, was used in the making of medicines for rheumatism and gout. In addition to detailed instructions as to how the herb should be collected, washed and dried, there was a sombre warning at the end of the circular: 'children should be warned that Colchicum is a deadly poison.'[55]

School children were also required, amongst other things, to collect acorns, horse chestnuts and beechmast for pig feed, gather wool from barbed wire fences and blackberries and other fruit for the women's voluntary services. Many children found these tasks particularly arduous because they had already worked for two hours before beginning the school day. Claire Rayner recalled her time with a host in Devon:

Part of being their vaccie meant getting up at the crack of dawn or earlier to wash eggs in cold water, and bundle radishes, spring onions and carrots for market. All this before school and breakfast. It wasn't so bad in the summer, when there was chance of pinching a carrot or two to gobble, earth and all – I never seemed to have enough to eat – but in the winter months when it was dark in the morning and bitterly cold all there was to do was wash eggs, because the vegetable season was over ... I used to get dreadful chilblains, appallingly painful cold injuries on my hands and lips that would itch and hurt until I hardly knew what to do with myself.

Above: Many children were involved in the Dig for Victory campaign, which aimed to boost the nation's fresh food supply.

And then there was the day I dropped three eggs and was sent to school with a black eye. Not that any of the staff noticed. It was probably easier that way.[56]

For children such as the young Claire, evacuation was a living nightmare, working from dawn until dusk with little or no recompense. Some indication of just how much school children contributed to the war effort can be gleaned by the reaction of farmers to government plans to revoke the Defence Regulations after the war. Even before the plans were officially announced, letters of protest were bombarding Westminster. The following letter written in 1953 from the president of the National Farmers Union to Sir Thomas Dugdale is just one example:

It has just been reported to me that the government have decided to allow Regulations 29 and 30 of the Defence (Agriculture and Fisheries) Regulations 1939, to lapse on the 10 December 1953. These, of course, are the Regulations which permit the employment, under safeguards, of children in agricultural work and have made it possible in particular for children to be engaged in term time, under exemptions granted by the local education authority, on potato picking. You will know that in fact a very large acreage of potatoes for many years past has in fact been harvested by school children under these arrangements. The information has been communicated to us under a pledge of confidence until it is publicly announced by the government next month; but I felt bound to write to you at once to let you know that we regard this decision as one likely to create a very serious situation as respects next year's potato crop, particularly since many farmers are now ordering, or have already ordered, their seed and other requisites for next year's crop.[57]

According to official sources, children in some areas like Durham were responsible for picking 59 per cent of the potato crop every year.[58] It was not surprising therefore, that farmers objected to the withdrawal of term time child labour. By now however, the Board of Education had become the Ministry of Education with more status and political power and there was no disputing the fact that Regulation 29 and 30 of the 1939 Act had disrupted school work for long enough. Not before time the government was also taking a stronger stance towards child protection. The Curtis Report in England and Wales and the Clyde Report in Scotland had uncovered a catalogue of war time child abuse that had shocked the nation. Speaking in the House of Commons on 19 November 1946, Mr Nicholson, Conservative MP for Farnham, made an emotive appeal for urgent child care reform, stating that:

He could scarcely believe that the government was unaware of the deep sense of disquiet felt by every section of the population as a result of the Curtis Report... A melancholy and ugly picture had been presented and the whole volume was a sorry condemnation of the inspection system and of the Ministry of Health which had received the inspectors' reports and had done nothing about them.[59]

The Curtis and Clyde Reports laid the blame for the shocking ill-treatment of children at the doors of both central and local government. Furthermore, they established that divided responsibility within official departments and a general apathy towards the care of children lay at the crux of child neglect. For many within the House of Commons and the House of Lords the Reports confirmed what they had already suspected, namely that, with regard to children things had gone very badly wrong during the war years. In response to the shocking revelations, the government did legislate with a degree of urgency and a new children's Act was introduced in 1948. The Act established a system of local authority Children's Departments and Children's Officers. All Children's Officers were required to undergo training and the Home Office assumed responsibility for the child care service. As the MP for Bradford North explained:

The object of this central authority is to make sure that never again shall a child die of cruelty or neglect, as did Dennis O'Neill, and that never again shall a child suffer from the confusion and muddle in administration.[60]

In effect, the Act amounted to a complete 'U' turn in government policy. From delegating welfare to local authorities the new legislation shifted the emphasis and responsibility back to central government. The appointment of the Home Office as overseer of a new welfare system was an attempt to fortify the Act with a strong political backbone. The local authorities were not even allowed to design their own child care committees under the Act, nor appoint Children's Officers without the approval of the Secretary of State, emphasizing the move towards central control.

For abused evacuees however, this was all too little too late. One of the teachers involved in the evacuation process described the Act as: 'a bit like shutting the stable door after the horse has bolted.'[61] Throughout the war there were evacuees who had been billeted with criminals, abortionists, prostitutes, paedophiles, violent brutes, vicious degenerates and incompetents. Most of these bear the emotional scars to this day. As Claire Rayner observed, 'evacuation shattered families and exposed children to all sorts of cruelty. Some of this was perhaps worse than being bombed in London'[62]

Endnotes

1 Letter to author September 11, 1999
2 Starns, P. & Parsons, M., 'Against Their Will: The Use and Abuse of Children During The Second World War' in Marten. J, (eds.), Children and War (2002). See also the oral history tapes which are held in the Centre for Evacuee Studies, University of Reading.
3 Reward is defined in the Act as 'any payment or gift of money or money's worth, or any promise to give money's worth irrespective of whether there is any intention of making profit.'
4 'Instructions for the Guidance of Regional and Local Committees' issued by the Executive Committee for The Movement for the Care of Children from Germany, May 1940, p. 17. Herefordshire County Police? Office J65/1406
5 Ibid, p. 16
6 Oral history interview Cambridge University evacuation project, A. S. July 1999
7 Extracts from Fen Drayton Council School Log Book, 29 & 30 October 1941, Cambridgeshire County Record Office C/ED/66C/4
8 Ibid. 25 October
9 Log Books included in this analysis were obtained from Cambridgeshire, Herefordshire, Worcestershire, Wiltshire, Nottinghamshire, Cheshire, Leicestershire and Lancashire.
10 Rayner. C, How Did I Get Here From There? (2003) p. 79
11 Benton. M-R, Family Values, Early stages of a touring actor (1998) p. 25
12 Oral history interview Cambridge University evacuation project, L.F. July 2000
13 Interview with Enid Philpott, 2016
14 Oral history interview Cambridge University evacuation project, S. H. June 1999
15 Ibid.
16 Rayner, C,.How Did I Get Here From There? (2003) p. 64-65
17 Ibid., p. 65
18 Flanagan, J., Tears Twice Over: My Experience as an Evacuee in Cheshire and Somerset, unpublished memoir, undated
19 Oral history interview Cambridge University evacuation project – M. K. April 1999
20 Oral history interview Cambridge University evacuation project – B. J. April 1999
21 Oral history interview Cambridge University evacuation project – A. H. April 1999
22 Oral history interview Cambridge University evacuation project – A. S. April 1999
23 Oral history interview Cambridge University evacuation project – M. L. April 1999
24 Oral history interview Cambridge University evacuation project – J. G. April 1999
25 Oral history interview Cambridge University evacuation project – A. S. April 1999
26 Oral history interview Cambridge University evacuation project – K. H. April 1999

27 Oral history interview Cambridge University evacuation project – L. S. April 1999

28 Oral history interview Cambridge University evacuation project – J. N. April 1999

29 Parsons, M, *Waiting to go Home* (1999) p. 100

30 Ibid. p. 102

31 Starns, P. & Parsons, M.,*Against their Will: the use and abuse of children during the Second World War,* in Marten, J (eds) Children and War (New York University Press), (2002), p. 272

32 Oral history interview conducted by the BBC, A. W. July 1999

33 Oral history interview, Cambridge University evacuation project – S. D., June 1999

34 Freedland, M. Michael Caine (1999) p. 20

35 Ibid p. 21

36 Ibid

37 Ibid

38 Ibid p. 20

39 Benton, M., *Family Values Early stages for a touring actor* (1998) p. 30

40 Sharp, P.,'The Fight for Child Labour' *Education Journal,* Vol LXXVI no. 1961, 9 August 1940, p. 91

41 Hall, W.,*Arise Sir Michael* (2000) p. 18

42 Ibid

43 Fulbourn Chronicle, 20 September 1940, p. 4

44 National Archive/MAF/38/35 Report of the International Labour Office, Permanent Agricultural Committee, 1st Session: Geneva, 1 February 1938

45 Ibid

46 The only complete legislation with respect to children working in agriculture was introduced by the Austrian government in 1935. The Austrian Act of 13 July 1935 involved a system of work cards for children aged fourteen years and over. No work card was issued if the work was considered to present a physical or moral danger.

47 Sharp, P.,'Children on the Land' *Education Journal,* vol LXXIX, no 2035, 15 May 1943, p. 385.

48 Ibid

49 Middlesex and the Defence Regulations Education Journal, vol. LXXIX, no. 2055, 29 May 1942, p. 431.

50 Zelizer, V., quoted by L. Ossian, in *'Too Young for a Uniform'* in J. Marten, (eds) *Children and War,* (2002), p. 256.

51 Intercommunication, letter from Mr Eddie Williams of Blackwood to the editor, Education Journal, vol LXXIX, o. 2055, 29 May 1942, p. 432

52 Fletcher, R., *'Helping Food Production'*, Littleport and Bethnal Green School Magazine Autumn term 1940, p. 3

53 Education Journal vol. LXXIX, no, 2055, 29 May 1942, p. 432

54 Ibid

55 Ibid

56 Address to local education authorities, teachers and youth organizations at Southpark High School Lincoln, 24 September 1941. *Education Journal* vol LXXVII, no. 2021, 3 October 1941

57 Sheffield City Archives ref: CA/77/1/1/1

58 Rayner, C.,*How did I get here from there?* (2003), p. 66

59 National Archive MAF/186/16 Letter to Sir Thomas Dugdale from the President of the National Farmers Union 27 October 1953.

60 National Archive MAF/186/16 Letter to H. H. Parker at the Ministry of Agriculture and Fisheries from J. Phillips, Assistant Secretary of the National Farmers Union, 26 October 1953

61 *The Guardian*, 20 November 1946, p. 6

62 Handard Parliamentary Debates 5th Series, 7 May 1948, col, 1647

63 Oral history interview Cambridge University evacuation project, G.D. July 1999.

64 Rayner, C., *How did I get here from there?* (2003), p. 5

Chapter 5
Homecoming and Evacuation's Legacy

On 8 May 1945, Britain celebrated Victory in Europe (VE Day) and a few months later on 15 August, Victory in the Far East (VJ Day), although officially the end of the war in the UK was on 2 September. However, long before the celebrations had got under way, and despite an official 'Stay Put' campaign, a tidal wave of evacuees had returned to the cities and hopes for an orderly and calm restoration to a sense of normality did not materialise. Designated trains were made available and free rail tickets were distributed to evacuate those wanting to collect or accompany them on their return home. But the need to identify children from thousands of reception areas and return them to their original place of departure was not an easy task. Besides which, over half the number of known evacuees had already returned home under their own steam by March 1945. A year later, on 31 March 1946, the government's evacuation scheme officially drew to a close. At this time, 3,000 still remained in the reception areas

Video 32 Jean and Ray Banks: *Homecoming*

with their host parents and a further 2,000 were housed in children's homes.[1] Some had been deserted by their parents, some had been made homeless and others simply had no homes to go to.

The sustained bombing of major cities had resulted in a severe housing crisis that was going to take some time to resolve. A shortage of materials and black-market building compounded the problem.

For all its celebrations of victory, Britain continued to experience wartime austerity. Rationing remained a feature of everyday life until 1954, and food shortages resulted in endless high street queues. The following poem written about a high street grocer and his shop in the run up to Christmas 1945 amusingly captures the spirit of the time:

Let us sing of the glories of Christmas in the days we remember afar,
'Ere peace and goodwill had been banished by the shadowy spectre of war.

When Sid was a real Father Christmas, in his brightly lit Eign Street Bazaar, surrounded by satisfied housewives, who had come in from near and far. When his ticker beat time out correctly, and his critics said, 'he's got a nerve!' As the graph of his sales went a-soaring in a beautiful positive curve. When his food store was crowded with turkeys, ducks, geese, tender chickens and ham, and nuts, figs and dates, with bananas. And melons, and strawberry jam. Ah, those were the days for the housewife, when shopping was easy and free, when a pound note was worth twenty shillings and she could buy lashings of tea.

When points and the coupons we treasure were horrors that we never knew. When we saw what we wanted and got it without having to stand in a queue.

But now, though we get higher wages, our income we watch with concern, as it quickly gets smaller and smaller since all of us pay as we earn.

The children can't hang up their stockings, for the shops are depleted of toys, the girls have no tea-sets nor dollies no meccano and trains for the boys.

And Dad cannot get any whisky to drink to a Happy New Year.

His cigars are still out in Havana and there's hardly a hop in the beer.

Yet let us take heart and be merry, for although we are still in a mess, We at least shall celebrate Christmas far better than Goering or Hess.

And if poultry is out of the question Mr Partridge still has plenty of fish To fill up 'the great open spaces' on our Christmas austerity dish.[2]

John Virgo – evacuated from Southampton to Higher Loop Farm, Lytchett Matravers, Dorset, June 1940
Autumn passed into winter and Christmas was my first away from my family, but my new family ensured that I had some nice presents, including a big metal aeroplane!

As the process of post war reconstruction began against a background of obliterated streets, bereaved and confused families attempted to regain a sense pre-war unity. Victory had been achieved but at what cost? What were the short- and long-term effects of evacuation on post-war Britain? How had the experience affected society as a whole, and those who were directly involved? Evacuation had raised the profile of the child but for how long?

The traditional historical debate has centred on whether or not the process of evacuation did prompt a re-evaluation of society in terms of social class.

However, this preoccupation with social class has obscured the more fundamental changes that occurred in other aspects of society as a result of evacuation. Certainly, in the immediate post war period, socialist notions of egalitarianism were not lost on the general public. However, actions always speak louder than words and political rhetoric was not always supported by action. For instance, the framework of private education and health-care remained firmly intact despite the implementation of wide-ranging reforms in state education and health-care. While there was some political commitment to an egalitarian society in theory, this same commitment could not be wholeheartedly transformed into practice. The main obstacle to this transformation was a political desire to at least maintain some semblance of class boundaries. Indeed, once hostilities had ceased, the short-term effect of evacuation was to reinforce the social class system. Middle class families shored up their boundaries and reeled against what they deemed to be the physical and moral decadence of working-class lifestyles. The various homecoming experiences of evacuees also confirmed that the British class system was very much alive and kicking. One woman recalled how a lady who lived at a manor house on the edge of a village in Somerset attended a church service and later remarked to a member of the congregation:

> Now that the war is over won't it be wonderful to rid the village of grubby evacuees? It has been ghastly having to put up with them, but I suppose we all had to do our bit for the war.[3]

The lady in question had not actually housed any child evacuees grubby or otherwise, but claimed that she had felt obligated to offer accommodation to civil servants and army personnel.

A report by the Cambridgeshire Village Life Committee recorded with some relief:

> Evacuation has come and gone (except for a few who remain), leaving very conflicting impressions. If our villages have learnt something of the slum conditions in the towns, we hope that returning evacuees have happy memories of country and an understanding of what the country contributes to the life of the nation.[4]

While evacuation had not prompted any major ideological shift in political or public thinking with regards to social class, it had transformed society in practical ways. Of course, there were the obvious changes, such as a welfare system that had evolved almost by default as the desperate circumstances of evacuees created an awareness of extreme poverty. The Children's Act was yet another example of change that was directly linked to the experience of evacuees. However, there were also fundamental changes in society as a result of evacuation that were so subtle as to be completely overlooked. From 1939, in the reception areas at least, the upbringing of children was effectively handed over to teachers; and the education system assumed more responsibility for certain aspects of child rearing. Moreover, because of the six-year rupture of normal child-parent relationships thousands of parents had missed out on the parental experience, while some of their children were subjected to either inadequate or detrimental parental role models. These same children were later unable to develop the crucial parenting skills they needed to pass on to the next generation. It can also be argued that a cycle of abuse was created during the war from which Britain has never recovered. As Janine Turner has pointed out: 'the pattern is rarely broken. They, their children and their children's children become the abused and abusers of the future tomorrow, and tomorrow and tomorrow.'[5] Since these shifts happened gradually and at a basic level of society, they affected every family in Britain. Subsequently therefore, many children were brought up by insecure parents with unrealistic expectations of the education system.

As child guidance clinics expanded to deal with children traumatised by evacuation, the government also changed its policy towards working women. Mothers were now told in no uncertain terms that it was psychologically damaging to their children for them to leave home and go out to work. It should be pointed out, though, that this change in policy direction was prompted more by a concern to boost the birth rate than by a genuine desire to meet the psychological needs of children. Despite government propaganda, however, some women who had gained a degree of independence during the war years were not easily persuaded to move back into their homes and stay there. The government responded by cutting the number of nursery places, while the BBC attempted to woo women back to the kitchen by the introduction of *Women's Hour*. Despite a general public mood of optimism for change, therefore, large sections of Britain's post-war population were encouraged to return to the familiar features of pre-war Britain. Change was also curtailed by financial constraints. The post-war Labour government was confronted with a precarious balance of payments deficit and an unexpected termination of the American lend-lease programme. This situation was compounded by the emergence of Cold War politics, which demanded a substantial increase in defence spending. Eventually, Britain managed to secure a new loan from America but the terms were restrictive and the interest payments crippling.[6]

Notwithstanding substantial government reform measures in certain key areas of society, such as health and welfare, and education, at a grass roots level change was thwarted by traditionalists who clung to old ideas and practices. The education system, for instance, reverted very quickly to a pre-war curriculum that was underpinned by a continued emphasis on citizenship. There were a few areas of experimentation but faced with an onslaught of emergency trained teachers, hurriedly recruited to cope with shortages, existing teachers took refuge in the tried and tested methods of a bygone age. The Headmaster of Aston Commercial School, Mr Flack, writing in 1949, observed that:

> One of the best ways to start an argument in a staff room is to speak in favour of 'activities' or the 'project' method. Usually most of the heat is generated on the opposition side, for it is often assumed that these new ideas contribute nothing of value, that they waste time, and that in consequence many children leave school without a sound knowledge of the basic subjects of the curriculum.[7]

Amidst this general trend of retrenchment however, it was possible to detect some undercurrents of change. Professional retrenchment was to some extent counteracted by innovative measures designed to support the education system. Education authorities, such as Birmingham and Bristol for example, were way ahead of the field in terms of spearheading a national schools careers service. This innovation represented a major change for British school children. Before 1939, children had approached their parents for careers advice, but the disruption of parent child relationships during the war had undermined this usual source of information and prompted a totally new educational field.

A careers officer working in Bristol recalled her initial work in the new service:

> One of the first tasks was to convince some parents that they had set their sights too high for their son or daughter. We had a period of full employment and what with the Butler Education Act and the New National Health Service there was an air of optimism about the future. Unfortunately not all children were capable of taking full advantages of the opportunities available. Really the war had severely damaged education and some children were totally illiterate, it was difficult to find jobs to suit some of them. Then we had the immigrant population and language difficulties to deal with. We were lucky in Bristol because the Wills tobacco factory took a lot of them and they treated their youngsters well so that made my job a lot easier.[8]

In addition to the new careers service, there were also developments in educational psychology and improvements in the school medical service. The most important influence of evacuation on education, however, did not become apparent until the 1960s and emerged in the form of teachers who had previously been evacuees. They had been taught in a variety of ways and were keen to implement new ideas based on their experiences as pupils. A Headmaster from Liverpool remembered his enthusiastic approach with some glee:

> *The first thing I did was get rid of streaming. There seemed to be a general expectation that children in the higher streams would do well and the others would be left to rot. Teachers concentrated on the two highest streams and gave very little effort to those lower down in the pecking order. Once streaming was abolished it was great, like an exciting free-for-all where children could develop at their own pace and help each other along the way. I also insisted that all the classes were taught outside when the weather was good and took every opportunity to arrange field trips. My education during the war was by no means perfect but it was always interesting and we were hardly ever classroom based because there was never any room for us interlopers. But it did show me that there was a different and more exciting way to teach and I was determined to introduce new methods as soon as I got the chance.[9]*

A headmistress from Birmingham recounted a similar story:

> *There were a lot of new ideas around in the 1960s and apart from myself several of my colleagues held very liberal views. Most of us had received our education during the war years. It was a disruptive education of course but when I became one of those emergency trained teachers I knew then that I wanted to teach how I was taught as an evacuee. It was a lot freer then I think. I am pretty sure that my training would never have survived the OFSTED inspections of today but I managed. Then, eventually, I found myself in a position where I could make some changes and I was like a new broom sweeping clean across the school.[10]*

Although the state system was not renowned for its innovative teaching methods, a few schools had gained a reputation for being experimental even before the war. When an evacuee returned to England from Canada with her sister Suzette, she was astounded at the radical nature of one in particular.

> *We were advised that Dartington Hall had a reputation as an experimental progressive form of education, and without questioning that description further parents thought that after the rather free way of life in Canada, it might suit Suzette rather well. In any event in August we set off for Devon by train, having made appointment for a certain morning with the headmaster, Mr W. B. Curry. We were not aware of the*

specific nature of the school or what kind of experiments it professed. If we had known, we probably wouldn't have gone... Mr Curry conducted the interview by outlining the purpose and functions of the school, according to his philosophy of freedom and self-government: co-education, co-habitation might be a more accurate word, involving full participation by students in every facet of life. At that time little importance was given to preparing them for the School Certificate. Scholastics and academics were secondary to arts, and free expression and individual development of each child.

After this introductory talk Mr Curry offered to show us around the school buildings and groups. It was a beautiful place, in a lovely setting. The open-air swimming pool was on the tour of course, and here the significance of what we had been hearing about the school's philosophy, was borne out in no unmistakable terms. At one end of the pool were the changing rooms and it struck us immediately that there was no separate accommodation for boys and girls. My mother queried the reason for, what seemed to her, these very inadequate arrangements, and it was then Mr Curry explained that it was customary for the children to swim in the nude, that it was the policy not to have segregation of the sexes in any way, and therefore it was totally unnecessary to have separate changing rooms.

My mother ventured to voice her concern that she didn't think her fourteen-year-old daughter would like swimming without her bathing costume. Mr Curry assured her that it would be quite permissible for her to wear it, but said he felt sure, she would begin to feel strange as the odd one out, and freely divest herself of it. After this startling revelation we bade our goodbyes and on reporting all this to my father, with a certain amount of merriment I might add, it was decided that Dartington Hall, or perhaps any co-ed boarding school, was not the answer. [11]

Not all evacuees returning from the Dominions were faced with such radical expressions of education, most were confronted by a rigid and inflexible education system which offered little in the way of opportunity when compared to their host countries. Some were so disillusioned by the educational restrictions on their return to Britain that they opted to emigrate at the first opportunity. Edward Stoye was one such case:

I went back to England before entering High School. I arrived just in time to sit the eleven plus exam. Needless to say I didn't do very well and was relegated to a secondary modern school. Such a placing excluded me from attending university or even a technical college, of course. My parents appealed but got nowhere. I remembered being given an intelligence test by the principal of the school. He heckled me as I did the test and naturally I didn't do it well. I think my parents' experience with the English education system was the reason we all moved to Canada in 1947. Here I did go to university.[12]

In fact, the secondary modem system of education did not preclude the possibility of admission to university or technical college, but it did make the process more difficult. For many evacuees returning from overseas however, the education system was not the only aspect of British society that failed to live up to expectations. The personal recollections and reflections of their individual homecomings emphasized the stark contrast in living standards between Britain and other members of the Commonwealth.

When I arrived back from Canada there was nothing left of our street. The whole family had to go and live at my Aunt's house because at least it was still standing even if it looked like it should have been condemned. Everything about England, even the people, seemed drab and shabby compared with what I'd been used to. I felt as though I didn't belong anymore; six years is a long time out of a child's life. I never properly fitted in with the family again. I couldn't even understand my parents' accent.[13]

We'd had plenty of food in Australia and lots of open spaces to play. People seemed more relaxed and friendly. When I got back home everyone seemed weary and there was no nice food, you know – no treats or anything. I began to feel very guilty because my family had had such a bad time and I had been quite unaware really. I didn't want to tell them how happy I'd been when I was away so I didn't tell them anything at all. They just thought I'd become a moody teenager.[14]

Nothing was like I remembered it. My elder brother had been killed in the RAF, there was no sign of any of my friends and I felt permanently lost. I still do, it's a feeling that has never gone away. It's as though I am living on shifting sand all the time.[15]

Jewish children evacuated under the Kindertransport would also be able to sympathise with this shifting sand metaphor. Fred Barschak describes:

The trauma of re-establishing some infrastructure of normality in a strange land, with new families, however sympathetic and kind, with the child enjoying a dubious status, neither a temporary guest, nor adopted, a sort of twilight world of not knowing where she or he belonged, which

was a state of being that was to last, for some, all their lives.[16]
Overseas evacuees had received official assistance in order to adjust to new lifestyles in strange and foreign countries. But for many the trauma of their homecoming was probably worse than their departure, since there were no attempts to ease these children back into their homeland. On their return, they were simply expected to adapt and get on with everyday living as though the previous six years had been a mere hiatus in their upbringing.

There was some evidence, however, that local social service departments provided at least an initial service in terms of meeting children from ports and escorting them to their various destinations. The following letter was written by G. L. Boyle in 1944 to Bristol Social Services Department to express his thanks for his children's safe escort:

> *Dear Sir,*
>
> *I cannot say how grateful my wife and I are for the great service you rendered us when the children arrived back in England. It was quite an experience for them both and had it not been for your kind offices when they landed at Bristol I feel sure they would have suffered considerable distress of mind. I would also like to thank the gentleman who, at a moment's notice, accompanied the children to Paddington. It was an example of real Christianity in practice.*[17]

Not all return journeys were predictable and some children had no idea when or how they would reach England, or indeed where they would arrive. Parents would often need to contact several possible points of arrival in the hope of obtaining assistance for their onward journeys. Officials at the Ministry of Health Regional Office in Bristol wrote the following vague letter to the Director of Bristol Social Services:

> *Dear Sir,*
>
> *Anthony and David Carr*
>
> *Information has been received that the above mentioned boys who were privately evacuated are expected to arrive in this country from the USA in the near future, probably on a naval craft. No information is available as to the port at which the boys may arrive, but if they should arrive at your port I shall be glad if you will arrange for them to be met and if necessary provided with accommodation temporarily. The parents are anxious to meet the boys at any London station indicated, but do not want them to be sent to Windsor by any other route. Any expenses incurred on the boys behalf should be claimed from the parents and no doubt you will inform this office on the event of their arrival.*[18]

Those returning from overseas frequently found it difficult to readjust to home life, but they were not the only ones to express feelings of dislocation and isolation. Domestic evacuees returning to cities from the reception areas also viewed their homecomings with mixed feelings.

I felt like a fish out of water when I got back to Liverpool. I'd had six years of wandering down country lanes and playing in fields. I'd had a nasty experience in my first billet but it was sorted out pretty sharpish and I was happy as Larry after that. The first thing that struck me about Liverpool was the narrowness of streets and the lack of green places. I remember thinking: I can't stay here forever. I was desperate to get back to Wales.[19]

I was only evacuated when the doodlebug came so I spent most of the war in London at any rate. Anyway, when the doodlebug hit the streets I was sent to Somerset. I was very badly treated. I never forgave my mother for sending me away. I'd been with her nearly all through the war and then she went and sent me away. I never understood why, and I never trusted her again.[20]

John Bowen was eleven when he returned to Southampton from five years as an evacuee in the countryside of Somerset.
It was horrible – coming home to a slum. We didn't have much when we left but it was what we knew, but coming back it was worse than ever. The house next door had been hit by incendiaries and burned down and our house was damaged when they tried to put the fire out. It was still like that when I left in 1950.

John Henry Grant Evans was born in Southampton in 1928 and was evacuated to Castle Cary with his friend John Bath. On his return to his home city, he remembers:
Both mothers came down to collect John and I to take us back to Southampton and after a long train journey we arrived back at the Terminus Station in the dark. We walked to the bus stop at Houndwell and all I could see were bombed ruins with white painted fencing to keep one clear of the bomb damage. I kept asking my Mother 'Where are we?' I did not recognize Southampton. While I would have preferred to stay at home with my family, I realized it saved my parents a lot of worry knowing that I was in a reasonably safe place.

Above: Mrs Carroway owned a big house, with staff,
something Doris Nicholson was not used to.

Doris Nicholson, nee Cook, was nine when she was evacuated from
Woodford, Ilford, Essex to a well-to-do home in Taunton, Somerset, where
she lived in a household with domestic staff. Coming home was difficult.
*It was not really a good homecoming. I had a sister. She was alright. She
was pretty but we never got on. We were chalk and cheese, her and me.
She was older than me. We just tolerated each other. She was too old to
be evacuated. She was different. I think that was the difference. I went
and lived with that older lady during the war and it made a difference.
I was the only child there and I suppose that was what it was. I found it
difficult to fit in with my sister.*
Interview with Doris Nicholson, October 2016

It was not uncommon for returning evacuees to demonstrate resentment towards their parents. While many of the latter had accepted evacuation as a means of saving their children's lives, the children themselves had viewed the process as an act of abandonment.

'Pat' was just three years of age when she went with her mother and Aunt Glad to Llandilo in Glamorganshire, Wales.

We finally arrived at Mr and Mrs Evans' house. Aunty Glad disappeared to live at another house and I don't remember seeing her again when I was in Wales. The house [I was living in] did not have any electricity or running water. Mr and Mrs Evans had a large family – only one girl, called Morfydd, and several boys. The main room was the huge kitchen with a large table and several chairs. The whole household were Welsh speaking, only speaking English to officials and people like the doctor. The house was in complete contrast to our home in London with all the goods and services that one would expect in a town. This house was in the depth of the Welsh countryside. I cannot recall a shop or anything really outside the Evan's family, although I do remember going to school and singing Welsh songs.

My mother, I suppose, did not see a role for herself in such a place and, having established that Mrs Evans would look after me like a member of her family, quickly went back to London and took up factory work. I settled down in Wales but it was a steep learning curve for me at just three-years-old. Mrs Evans loved me but I'm afraid the children hated me… I remember them teasing me an awful lot and I think I was very unhappy. I had to learn Welsh quickly to try to fit in with the rest of the family but when my parents came to visit me they could see that I was unhappy and took me home. I think I was in Wales for less than a year but it ruined my relationship with my mother. I could never forgive her for leaving me on my own there. Of course, as an adult I can understand her feelings and she was doing exactly what the war government wanted, but as a child I did not know why she went out of my life so suddenly. I know that I would never leave a child of mine. Now, as an adult, I feel sorry for my mother in such a situation. As a child I did not have that facility of looking back.[21]

The view that children had been abandoned was fuelled by unjust allegations that were made during the war. These allegations claimed that working class mothers, and East End mothers in particular, had been desperate to get rid of their children. Claire Rayner was just one of a number of evacuees who wondered if there was any truth in these accusations pointing out that: 'It was a most cruel canard of the day that should never have been allowed utterance.'[22]

East End mothers were vilified throughout the war, along with others from working-class areas. Amongst other things, they were accused of being neglectful, foul mouthed, ungrateful and ignorant. The attempts of child welfare groups and other voluntary bodies to highlight the extreme poverty of some working-class families failed to exonerate working-class mothers. To some extent these otherwise well-meaning groups made the problem worse. Middle-class women, in particular, investigated the causes of poverty and were good at agitating for reform and welfare improvements. At the same time however, they were also good at pointing out the supposed virtues of the middle-class, and what they perceived to be the failings of working-class mothers. Furthermore, it is also clear that, in terms of achieving any influence, patronising attitudes and notions of good motherhood as defined by middle-class women, were not going to cut any ice with working-class mothers.

In reality, the only difference between working and middle-class mothers was the fact that the latter had better housing and more money. Neither was there much difference between city and rural areas when it came to the poverty stakes. Dramatic stories about poor, bad mannered and dirty city children who were riddled with lice may have made national headlines during the war but these same stories overlooked the poor, bad mannered and dirty children in rural areas, who were also riddled with lice long before a city child had ever set foot in a reception area. But, although the stories were often exaggerated, biased and inaccurate, they did succeed in raising the profile of the child within the community. More importantly they ensured that issues of child poverty and malnutrition were eventually tackled at the highest level. Welfare measures that were implemented in schools from 1941 onwards did bring about improvements in the post-war health of children. Psychologists, who had largely viewed evacuation as a great experiment, paid greater attention to the minds of children because of the disruption of so many mother and child relationships. Social workers, meanwhile, merely created a problem family out of a problem group.[23]

Yet the problem family was sometimes merely an unsupported family. Between 1946 and May 1955, the number of married women in gainful employment rose two and a quarter million to three and three quarter million,[24] though by no means all of these were mothers. The government had attempted to resolve labour shortages by immigration alone but this policy had not entirely bridged the gap. Thus, central government officials actively began to encourage women to enter the workplace. When women were required to work in wartime, nursery places were made available, and evacuation had formed an essential part of the childcare framework. In the 1950s, many local authorities had substantially reduced their nursery provision and once again the neglect of children became headline news. Working class mothers who were often forced out to work by financial circumstances, were accused of turning their children into 'latch key kids'. Speaking in the House of Commons Mr Pardoe, a Liberal MP, stated:

> The employment in industry of women, particularly housewives and mothers, of young children, presents a problem. Not only do we want to bring back those qualified as doctors and teachers – the need is obvious – but we want to bring women into employment in the whole length and breadth of British industry. We all know about 'latch key' children and we don't want to encourage that sort of thing. We should ensure that industry is able to adapt itself to the problems of housewives and mothers of young children.[25]

Politicians debated the issues of childcare at length but no effective action was taken. Furthermore, while employed working-class mothers shouldered the blame for their problem families; many evacuees were labelled as problem children. Disruptive and anti-social behaviour, sullenness and withdrawal were all manifestations of the emotional trauma caused by evacuation. Feelings of bitterness, anger and resentment were carried into adulthood. Over eighty-five per cent of the evacuees interviewed for research purposes had suffered from one or more bouts of severe depression, panic attacks or other emotional disturbance. Some claimed that they suffered from extreme anxiety in situations that reminded them of their evacuation, such as when they embarked on train journeys or were required to pack a suitcase. [26]

Claire Rayner describes her experience:

> In the forties no one would have considered it possible for children to get depression. Actually, no one thought adults got it, apart from psychiatrists in the know, because the condition was never discussed in public. What would be the point, since there was no effective therapy for it? I was just labelled a problem child again, and harassed, punished and nagged, not only by my mother, in letters, but also by my teachers and hostel staff, who took their cue, naturally enough from the things my mother told them about me. I became ever more difficult and hell to have around. I look back on those years, which took me through almost to the end of the war, and wondered how I managed to live with myself, I was such a misery. [27]

Others have happier experiences and look back with a sense of fond nostalgia. As part of a research study, evacuees were asked what, if anything they had

Above: Women in factories had been an essential part of the war effort but less thought had been given to post-war childcare for women who continued to work.

learned from their evacuation. The following extracts are taken from their testimonies and reflect the wide range of personalities involved in the study:

I learnt that you couldn't trust anyone, my mother had said I going on a holiday, six years later I remember thinking some holiday that was! Every time anyone mentions the word holiday, I cast my mind back to that September day in 1939. I prefer to stay at home now.[28]

I think it made me more independent but I also think it had a very detrimental effect on my education. I learnt very easily and well until I was eleven and then, perhaps I shouldn't assume it, but if I had gone on to the next school everything would have just continued. But the breaking up of the formula of education, not having any proper schooling, I ended up with no qualifications whatsoever and everything in my life was fragmented then, and has been ever since.[29]

It gave me a tremendous love for the countryside. I've been back to the area where I was evacuated several times and I'm still in contact with my host family. I learnt a lot about flowers, plants and farm animals and I've tried to pass all this on to my children. I can walk along the riverside and pick out different birds and things and I know I wouldn't even have this interest if I'd not been evacuated.[30]

It made me a nervous wreck. I am a very clingy and anxious person and I don't think I was like that before the war. I was evacuated three times and each time I just remember this tight feeling in my stomach as though I was going to be sick. Even now if I have to do anything out of the ordinary I get the same feeling.[31]

I loved every minute of it, the trees, the lanes, the big farmhouse and the sounds of the country. As soon as I was able to get a job and a place to live in the country I did. I was glad to see the back of city life. My eldest brother was killed during the war and another brother Richard was injured, I was the only one to come through unscathed and I was very grateful to the family that looked after me, they were pretty simple folk but I've got no complaints. I learnt that people could be very kind.[32]

I suffered unbearable teasing and torment from other children as a vaccie. I felt very frightened being away from my parents. In the end my mother came and got me because I stopped eating and began sleep walking down the road every night. I learnt that being with your own family is very important and I am probably over protective with my own children now.[33]

I was billeted with a musical family and learnt to play the piano. They gave me a life-long interest in classical music. My mother thought it was wonderful because she thought I could get a job playing in an East End pub after the war. I didn't though. I couldn't face playing the likes 'On Mother Kelly's Doorstep' and 'Knees up Mother Brown.' My mother had never heard of Handel, she said classical music was too fancy for the likes of us.[34]

I met my husband during my time as an evacuee in Kettering. He had a very good billet while mine was not so good. He used to bring me food and listen to my horror stories. We kept in touch and later married. I learnt that Kettering was a place where they made shoes and boots but not much else. The people generally were okay. I think that I was unlucky with my billet but there were a lot who were worse off than I was.[35]

It made me stand on my own two feet from an early age. I was scared of the new surroundings at first but once I got used to everything it was all right I suppose. I quickly realized that adults took very little notice of what children thought or felt and I decided I had to make my own decisions and keep them to myself. I suppose I was what people nowadays would call insular but evacuation made me grow up. I learnt to take responsibility for myself because nobody else was interested.[36]

Looking back over the years it seems like another lifetime. I had a terrible time in Wales but at least I've lived to tell the tale.[37]

The latter sentiment is echoed by numerous ex-evacuees. There is no doubt that in the final analysis, the British government's policy of evacuation did save some lives. Moreover, the acknowledgement of this fact has been a consolation for all evacuees, particularly for those who were ill-treated. But, as the late Baroness Blackburn, Barbara Castle, pointed out in 1999 'there was no need for any of it, it was all unnecessary.' According to the Baroness, the government could, and should, have constructed adequate civil defence buildings in the first place.[38] The construction of deep underground shelters for every major city was rejected on financial grounds. There were also fears that the working class might disappear into them for the duration of the war. It is possible that had these shelters been built however, more lives might have been saved without the disruption of family ties. The fact that they were not built lends more weight to the argument that evacuation was more about obtaining maximum labour output from the population than providing adequate protection from the enemy. With mothers working in city factories and their children working on the land, the government managed to keep the war effort on track. Clearly, this argument offers no consolation to evacuees whatsoever, except perhaps for the knowledge that they were not only victims of war but active participants in an eventual British victory.

Endnotes

1 Packham, J., *Aspects of Social Policy the Child's Generation: Childcare Policy from Curtis to Houghton*, (1975), p. 21

2 Herefordshire County Record Office ref: K/38F/S4, *Hereford Times* 15 December 1945

3 Oral history interview Cambridge University evacuation project, D. G. June 1999

4 Cambridgeshire County Record Office ref: C30 Village Life Committee Report 1944

5 Turner, J., *Behind Closed Doors* (1988), p. 74

6 Starns, P., *March of the Matrons*, (2000), p. 99

7 Flack, W., in 'A Camp School Project Experiment' *Journal of the Institute of Education*, University of Birmingham, Session 1949 – 1950 Published in *Educational Review* Vol 2, No. 1, Oct 1949

8 Oral history interview Cambridge University evacuation project, M. J. May 1999

9 Oral history interview, K. M. Sept 2001

10 Oral history interview Cambridge University evacuation project K. M. April 1999

11 Imperial War Museum ref: 91/37/1

12 Lin. P., National Identity and Social Mobility: Class, Empire and the British Government Overseas Evacuation During the Second World War, *Twentieth Century British History*, vol 7, no. 3, 19996, p. 336

13 Oral history interview Cambridge University evacuation project S. G. May 1999

14 Oral history interview Cambridge University evacuation project A. H. April 1999

15 Oral history interview Cambridge University evacuation project G. S. May 1999

16 Barshank, F., Personal Accounts of the Kindertransport, xix, quoted in Stirling, E., 'Rescue and Trauma' in Marten, J. (eds), *Children and War* (2001), p. 69

17 Bristol County Record Office: letter to Bristol Social Services Department from G. I. Boyle of Cavendish Road, Cambridge, 19 November 1944

18 Bristol County Record Office: letter to the Director of Social Services from the

Ministry of Health Regional Office Bristol 8, 28 November 1944

19 Oral history interview BBC A. K. June 1999

20 Oral history interview BBC M. W. June 1999

21 Written statement by 'Pat', 2016

22 Rayner, C., *How did I get Here from There?* (2003), p. 52

23 MacNicol, J,. 'The Evacuation of School Children' in Smith, H., (eds) *War and Social Change* 1986 p 24

24 Titmuss. R., *Essays on the Welfare State,* 1958 p 102

25 Hansard Parliamentary Debates, 5th series 20th July 1966, col 754

26 Research conducted by psychologist Stephen Davies at the Princess Alexandra Hospital, Harlow Essex.

27 Rayner, C., *How did I get Here from There?* (2003), p. 94

28 Oral history interview Cambridge University evacuation project, A. W. August 2001

29 Oral history interview Cambridge University evacuation project, G. S. June 2001

30 Oral history interview Cambridge University evacuation project, E. G. July 2001

31 Oral history interview Cambridge University evacuation project, F. W. June 2001

32 Oral history interview Cambridge University evacuation project, K. I. September 2001

33 Oral history interview Cambridge University evacuation project, L. F. July 2001

34 Oral history interview Cambridge University evacuation project, T. N. June 2001

35 Oral history interview Cambridge University evacuation project, K. H. Sept 2001

36 Oral history interview Cambridge University evacuation project, J. M. July 2001

37 Oral history interview Cambridge University evacuation project, M. K. December 2002

38 Baroness Blackburn, Barbara Castle, interviewed for the BBC Radio 4 programme *Evacuee's Story* August 1999

Timeline

28th June 1938

The Anderson Committee seeks advice from Wing Commander R.V. Goddard, who advises the Committee not to evacuate children to the south or east of London. When the government's dispersal policy is introduced however, this advice is ignored.

31st August 11am 1939

Government issues order to evacuate forthwith, 47 percent of English school children and 38 percent of Scottish school children, along with younger children, their mothers and vulnerable adults are evacuated as Operation Pied Piper is implemented. Evacuees experience an ordered evacuation from major cities, but a chaotic reception in rural and small urban areas.

Defence regulations numbers 29 and 30 are issued, which allows children aged 13 and over to be exempt from school lessons in order to help with the war effort. In practice, children as young as five could be found working on the land throughout the war.

1st September 1939

The BBC Television signal is turned off for the duration of the war.

The Blackout begins.

3rd September 1939

Britain declares war on Germany.

24th November 1939

Over 90 per cent of evacuees have returned home, due to problems in reception areas, combined with a false sense of security engendered by the Phoney War. Some city schools are partially reopened.

Right: Tony Edwards with his sister Doreen in New Zealand

8th January 1940

Food rationing begins. Bacon, butter and sugar are the first items to be rationed.

16th February 1940

Government commissions several propaganda films aimed at keeping children in reception areas. These are *Westward Ho* and *Living with strangers*. In addition, several posters are produced to reinforce the same message. Board of Education issues memo to school inspectors.

April 1940

A fear of juvenile crime and rising levels of illiteracy prompt the Board of Education to reopen city schools. However, the rise in juvenile crime rates were most prevalent in the age group 14 to 18, when most children had left school.

Schools are encouraged to supply dinners for children, but children still had to surrender meat rations to school canteens.

May/June 1940

Second official wave of evacuation. The government introduces medical screening for all evacuees.

July 1940

In response to complaints about elitist child migration overseas, the government introduces the Children's Overseas Reception Board (CORB) scheme. Over 211,000 applications were received by CORB by the 4th of July. The scheme is eventually abandoned following the SS City of Benares disaster.

On the domestic front, there is a greater concern with child welfare and an urgent move to implement vaccination programmes. At this time, Diphtheria is the biggest threat to children, and was referred to as the child killer. Vaccination against Diphtheria became a government public health success story.

Video 33 John Hammond:
A National Service Messenger

16th August 1940

Croydon Aerodrome is bombed. As a result, Boy Scouts are asked to volunteer as fire watchers.

Over 50,000 Scouts were employed throughout the war in a range of National War Service roles including acting as messengers, firemen and stretcher bearers. They were also involved in the collection of essential supplies, such as paper.

DIPHTHERIA
is deadly

J·H·DOWD

protect your child by
IMMUNISATION

The best time is just before the first birthday

Ask at your Local Council Offices, School or Welfare Centre

ISSUED BY THE MINISTRY OF HEALTH AND THE DEPARTMENT OF HEALTH FOR SCOTLAND

Above: Diphtheria was a major threat during WW2, prompting
a successful government vaccination drive.

NATIONAL FIRE SERVICE

CERTIFICATE OF SERVICE

Name (in full) HAMMOND, John Richmond Paul

National Fire Service No. 531291   Date of discharge 3rd. May 1945

Rank on discharge PART-TIME MESSENGER

Cause of discharge REDUCTION IN ESTABLISHMENT

	WITH LOCAL AUTHORITY FIRE BRIGADE	WITH NATIONAL FIRE SERVICE
WHOLE-TIME SERVICE	from	from
	to	to
PART-TIME SERVICE	from	from 29. 10. 1943.
	to	to 3. 5. 1945.

3rd. May   19 45   Fire Force Commander.

Above: John Hammond's Certificate of Service in the National Fire Service.
More than 50,000 scouts gave invaluable war service.

Girl Guides became teachers and nursery nurses, whitewashed kerbs to help prevent accidents in the blackout, distributed gas masks and showed housewives how to construct an emergency oven from the bricks from their bombed-out homes.

29th August 1940
SS Volendam sails with 320 evacuee schoolchildren aboard.

30th August 1940
SS Volendam is hit by two torpedoes from the German submarine U-60. All 320 children are rescued.

Above: A group of children from *SS Volendam*.

7th September 1940

The first air raid of the London Blitz. London was to endure 57 consecutive nights of bombing.

17th September 1940

SS City of Benares is sunk after being hit by German submarine U-48. 77 of the 90 children on board perish.

Video 34 Dee Williams: *The first London air raid*

6th November 1940

12 children are killed in the daylight bombing raid on the Civic Centre, Southampton, when the Arts Block is hit by a 500lb bomb.

Video 35 Dee Williams: *The effects of the first air raid*

1941

The Means Test was replaced by a more lenient method of needs assessment.

There is an extension of a free school milk scheme. However, this becomes a health hazard for evacuees in the country because milk is not pasteurised in many rural areas, and many children contract bovine tuberculosis.

The government also introduces financial incentives to schools in order to extend the school meals service. Ministry of Food lays down guidelines for feeding young children.

Wartime inflation prevents the evacuation of children into the country because mothers can no longer afford billeting fees, and are reluctant to part with children's rations.

1942

The blueprint for the post war welfare state, devised by Sir William Beveridge, is published. People queued for hours to obtain the hugely influential Beveridge Report.

1944

The Butler Education Act is passed, which, amongst other things, raises the school leaving age to 15, with a provision to raise leaving age to 16 at a later date.

6th June 1944

D-Day

1945

In response to growing evidence of child abuse and the notorious case of Dennis O'Neil who was beaten to death by a Shropshire farmer, the government establishes committees of enquiry. These committees uncovered a catalogue of child abuse and reported their findings in 1946.

8th May 1945

VE Day – A Public Holiday to celebrate the end of the war in Europe.

2nd September 1945

VJ Day – the end of the war in Japan.

1948

In response to the Curtis report in England and the Clyde report in Scotland, the Children's Act of 1948 was passed. This single piece of legislation has since been globally described as the most humane Act ever passed by any parliament in any country.

The National Health Service and the Welfare State is introduced and subsequently improves the lives of all children.

Myths of the Blitz

Myth 1 Air Raid Precautions covered all sections of the population.
Fact Air Raid Precautions did not provide any protection for school children, and in some discussions about civilian protection, officials claimed that children were not part of the population!

Myth 2 There were no alternatives to the government's 'Dispersal Policy.'
Fact It was possible and highly desirable for city authorities to construct deep underground shelters, however, this option was considered to be too expensive. Military personnel also feared that deep shelters could become the focus for enemy gas attacks.

Myth 3 All city children were evacuated to reception areas for the duration of the war.
Fact During the first wave of evacuation only 47% of English schoolchildren were evacuated and 38% of Scottish school children. At no time during the war did children in reception areas outnumber those who remained in evacuation areas.

Myth 4 Evacuation was compulsory.
Fact Evacuation was never made compulsory, but billeting was compulsory.

Myth 5 Everyone pulled together during the blitz.
Fact Black market racketeering was rife and crime rates soared during the blitz. The murder rate went up by 22% between 1941 and 1945 and overall crime rose by 57% between 1939 and 1945.

Myth 6 There were very few cases of shell shock and psychological trauma during the Blitz.
Fact There were hundreds of cases of shell shock and 'nerves' during the blitz; but since all victims were sent to sector hospitals on the outskirts of cities these cases have been systematically overlooked.

Myth 7 Bombing was the biggest cause of absenteeism from work or school.
Fact Epidemics of tuberculosis, diphtheria, scarlet fever, measles and mumps were the biggest cause of absenteeism in the work place and class rooms.

Myth 8 All children evacuated to reception areas were healthier and happier than their city counterparts.
Fact The reverse is true. According to Ministry of Health and Board of Education statistics, children who remained in the evacuation areas grew to the desired weight and height, whilst those evacuated to the country had stunted growth rates. Children who remained in cities also experienced less psychological trauma.

Myth 9 All evacuated children left working class homes in cities to be housed in middle class homes in reception areas.
Fact There were hundreds of middle class children who were housed in working class homes in reception areas. Furthermore, working class homes housed over 80% of evacuees because middle and upper class homes in receptions areas were often commandeered to accommodate military personnel.

Myth 10 Householders in reception areas were happy to welcome those evacuated from danger areas.
Fact Undoubtedly some were happy to do so, however, there were cases of neglect, cruelty and abuse that, in some cases, led to the death of evacuated children.

Myth 11 Evacuee children were dirty, could not use a knife and fork, were not toilet-trained and brought disease to the reception area.
Fact Lack of understanding and empathy by some in the reception areas helped to spread such stories. There was as much disease in the reception areas as there was in the rest of the country.

Myth 12 Homecoming for evacuees was a joyful experience.
Fact This was undoubtedly true for the majority. However, for many, there was no home to come back to, or family to greet them. Further, many found that they no-longer had anything in common with those they left behind, making re-integration difficult.

Bibliography

Books

Brown, M. *Evacuees of the Second World War* (Shire Publications, Oxford, 2009)

Legg, P. *Crime in the Second World War: Spivs, Scoundrels, Rogues and Worse* (Sabrestorm Publishing, Sevenoaks, 2017)

Legg, P., *Voices of Southampton* (The History Press, Stroud, 2011)

Parsons, M., *I'll Take That One* (DSM publishing, Peterborough, 1998)

Parsons, M. & Starns P., *Evacuation the True Story* (DSM publishing for the BBC, 1999)

Smith, S. and Antram D., *Avoid being a Second World War Evacuee!* (Book House, an imprint of The Salariya Book Company Ltd, Brighton, 2003)

Starns, P., *The Evacuation of Children During World War II* (DSM publishing, Peterborough, 2004)

Starns, P., *Blitz Families* (The History Press, Stroud, 2012)

Starns, P., *Oceans Apart – Stories of overseas evacuees in World War Two* (The History Press, Stroud, 2013)

Websites

BBC: http://www.bbc.co.uk/history/ww2peopleswar/stories/52/a2077652.shtml

https://www.bbc.co.uk/news/magazine-11005064

Scouts: https://scouts.org.uk/news/2013/06/30-amazing-facts-about-scouts/

The British Evacuees Association: www.evacuees.org.uk

Photo credits

The Ed Thompson Collection Front cover, right

Legg Collection 8

Sabrestorm archives 11, 13, 108-109, 145

The 1940s Society (*www.1940.co.uk*)

38, 42, 45, 46, 125, 153,

John Bowen 24

Doris Nicholson 27, 141

Jill Simonds 28, 29

Dee Williams 30

John Hammond 32, 154

Peter Mooney 35

Alan Corbishley 65, 70, 71, 80, 81, 82, 83, 84, 85 (bottom), 86, 155

Tony Edwards 85 (top), 87, 88, 95, 151